BBQ Companion

BEN O'DONOGHUE

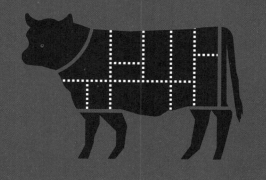

BBQ
Companion

BEN O'DONOGHUE

180+ Barbecue recipes from around the world

Hardie Grant

BOOKS

CONTENTS

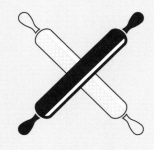

INTRODUCTION

There is no doubt that I love a barbecue. It's a style of cooking that continues to touch every culture, bringing people together all around the globe, and a social occasion that releases any sense of inhibition about ones ability to cook – everyone thinks they are a master!

According to the learned American gentleman Jonathan Daniels (1902–81), 'Barbecue is a dish which binds together the taste of both the people of the big houses and the poorest occupants of the back end of the broken-down barn.' Barbecues not only cross social and economic barriers, they also break down geographical and cultural boundaries. Every nation around the world has a form of barbecue, or certain types of food that are specifically cooked on one.

Barbecuing is a cooking technique – some would say an art form – that can be performed just about anywhere: in restaurants and backyards, in parks, at beaches or on street corners. The basic requirements are so simple, a barbecue can be fashioned from just about any raw materials you have to hand. I have seen shopping trolleys, terracotta planter boxes, metal garbage cans, roof sheeting, plough wheels – you name it. If you can build a fire in it, on it or under it, then you can have a barbecue. Whether you're talking about the hangi pits of New Zealand and Polynesia, the braziers in Morocco's souks, the blazing heat of a gaucho's grill, the pit masters of the southern states of America, the barbecue kings of the Antipodes or the street stallholders of Asia, the common denominator is always fire.

Fire, or more specifically, charcoal, lends a desirable flavour to food, and there is a primeval sense of security and accomplishment that comes from building a bonfire and cooking something in the flames. I well remember childhood memories of going down to the beach on early-morning fishing expeditions with my friends, building a fire and throwing our fresh catch onto the coals, the charred results leaving us utterly replete.

This initial foray into cooking led me down my professional path, and it was these childhood memories, combined with my more recent global wanderings and discussions with taxi drivers, kitchen porters and fellow barbecue aficionados, that prompted me to write this book.

Barbecue's origins lie in the Caribbean with the Indigenous Taíno People, whose barabicu was a form of pit cooking using green pimento tree branches and leaves, which imparted their flavour to the food. The word barbacoa was used by the Mesoamerican people of Mexico, and it is generally accepted that the word we use today made its way into popular usage via Texas, which was once part of Mexico.

In most parts of the world, to barbecue means to directly grill food over hot coals or gas. In the US, however, it refers to a form of slow, indirect cooking that's more in keeping with the tradition of pit cooking. Common to all methods is the fact that a barbecue is undeniably the most social and relaxing form of cooking and entertaining.

With the advent of new fuels and construction materials, the modern barbecue has come a long way from that classic backyard feature, the wood-burning barbecue – usually constructed from a couple of bricks and a rusty metal grill, or a 44-gallon barrel cut in half with thick metal mesh thrown over the top. These days, the barbecues we cook on are the compact designer models, ideal for apartment dwellers; hooded gas barbecues, with all their bells and whistles; kettle barbecues, with their rounded, domed design and useful lid; and those ineffectual electric barbecues found in public parks and picnic areas.

This book is a celebration of the barbecue and its global idiosyncrasies. All the classics are here, along with recipes I've re-invented and my own personal favourites. I have cooked or eaten all of these fabulous recipes while exploring and enjoying the diversity of the barbecue world. I hope you enjoy them as much as I do.

EQUIPMENT AND TIPS

The keys to a successful barbecue are preparation and some level of organisation. Whether you're attempting a major gastronomic event or just grilling a few steaks, there are a few things you need to remember.

Before you start thinking about whether you're doing T-bones, brisket, satay or squid, the first and most important thing to keep in mind is the golden rule: make sure you have enough fuel!

Other important rules when barbecuing are:

- Never leave your post
- Never hand the tongs to someone you can't trust
- When smoking, always remember: if you're looking, you're not cooking
- Also when smoking, what you need is a thin stream of smoke, not a great big cloud!

There are two basic methods of cooking on a barbecue:

Direct grilling involves exposing food directly to the heat source, using a skewer, grill or griddle. It's generally a fast way of cooking, and some people in the barbecue world consider it heresy!

Indirect cooking uses heat transfer via convection. Generally, the heat source is set away from the food, so it's a slower way to cook. Hot, smoky air passes through an enclosed container, whether using the hood of a gas barbecue, the lid of a kettle barbecue or, as in the US where this style of barbecuing is most common, an entire trailer converted into an oven that can hold a whole pig! Some barbecue experts consider the flavour and tenderness of meat cooked this way to be far superior to directly grilled meat.

FUEL

The most popular barbecues on the market are the hooded gas and charcoal-fuelled kettle models, which can be used to cook either indirectly or directly. The main difference between gas and charcoal fuel is the fact that gas 'burns colder' than charcoal. This means it provides a lower cooking temperature than briquettes, charcoal or wood, which with the addition of oxygen (i.e. a fan) can burn hot enough to melt metals! Purists will say that the flavour gained from the use of charcoal is far superior, both in terms of smokiness and the high heat that's achieved to sear the meat. Gas, on the other hand, is cleaner and far more time efficient. Now that a range of woodchips for flavouring barbecues is available, the argument for coal over gas has no clear winner, the choice being merely one of tradition or modernity.

So, you have your hardware – now what else do you need? You'll probably have most of the following in your kitchen, but remember that preparation is everything and can make or break your barbecue.

- Enough fuel (gas, charcoal or briquettes)
- Lightweight long-handled tongs
- A roasting fork for turning large joints of meat and lifting delicate fish fillets
- A long-handled spatula with a cutting edge
- Leather or thick gloves for handling hot metal
- Oven or barbecue mitts
- Plenty of paper towels
- A selection of sharp knives: a 23 cm chef's knife for chopping, a long-bladed boning knife for boning and filleting fish and meat, a paring knife for fruit and vegetables and a diamond steel to keep them sharp!
- A basting needle or brush (needles are good because they don't singe)
- Long metal skewers for kebabs and trussing poultry and fish
- Wooden skewers (these need to be soaked in water for an hour before using, so they don't burn on the grill)
- A fish basket for grilling whole fish

- Foil or qbags (an aluminium foil bag)
- Foil drip trays
- A roasting stand for large joints and birds
- A large, heavy cast-iron roasting tray
- A wire rack or cake rack to place over the roasting tray
- Selected woodchips (oak, mesquite, hickory, apple or your personal favourite), pre-soaked in water for an hour
- A bottle of water with a spray nozzle to help control woodchips when smoking
- A smoke box for giving your food that little extra touch of flavour when you're cooking with gas
- Absorbent material like fine gravel or kitty litter for the drip tray
- A fire extinguisher that's appropriate for the fire you're extinguishing – CO_2 is probably best
- A long-handled wire brush for cleaning
- Charcoal lighting chimney

BUILDING YOUR FIRE

Our hunter-gatherer ancestors had it tough. They had to carry fire with them while they travelled from one area to the next. What they would have given for a packet of firelighters and a box of matches!

The great convenience of gas is that you turn the bottle on, press the button and off you go. Gas barbecues need to heat up for 20–30 minutes, to help burn off any excess fat and dirt from the burners. Once clean, adjust the heat down a little and heat for a further 10 minutes for medium–hot; for medium–cool, reduce the heat a little more and heat for another 15 minutes. For simple grilling using gas, it's great to have high heat on one side graduating down to low on the other.

The ritual is slightly more involved if you have a charcoal barbecue. The fire needs to be built up and then allowed to burn down, requiring a preheating period of 35–45 minutes prior to cooking. A steady stream of fuel needs to be added during the cooking process, but the process of refuelling is not as simple as merely throwing more lumps of charcoal onto the fire. The smoke from coal is unclean when it initially starts to burn and can impart an unpleasant flavour to your barbecue. It's also hard to regulate the heat at first because in most cases the fire will cool prior to becoming hot again. The best way to maintain a constant heat using charcoal or briquettes is to use a fire box. It allows you to light new coals separately from your barbecue, quickly, evenly and efficiently, so when you add them they are hot enough to maintain your cooking temperature. Most modern coal barbecues have fire boxes.

With or without a fire box, the principle of lighting your coals is the same. Place your firelighters underneath your coals, so that the flames will rise up to light the coals evenly. The coals are ready for cooking when they are an even ashen white, which is when they are at their hottest. It takes up to 45 minutes to build an even coal base that is ashen white and hot enough to grill steaks or items that require fast high-heat cooking. Don't try to cook until the firelighters have burnt out or you will taint your food with the unpleasant fumes of accelerant. The way you arrange your coals will be determined by the method of cooking you wish to follow.

Direct grilling requires that you have a single base of evenly lit coals.

Indirect cooking requires that you separate the coals into either a single heat source away from the cooking area (i.e. a heat box outside the kettle or hooded area of the barbecue, as is common in the US) or into two smaller heat sources on either side of the barbecue grill (this method is most commonly used in kettle barbecues), separated by a drip tray. Don't open the lid too often as the heat will escape. For indirect cooking using gas, turn your outside burners to medium–low and the inner burners off.

Adding water to the drip tray when indirect grilling will help maintain moisture within the meat being cooked. This can also be achieved by using a spray bottle of liquid – for extra flavour you could try adding a spirit such as bourbon or whisky, or fruit juice.

MAINTAINING THE HEAT

Sometimes it pays to build your fire so that it graduates from a high, intense heat to a lower, more controllable heat. This can be achieved by pushing more coals to one side and a few to the other. Also, the closer the grill to the heat source, the higher the cooking temperature.

Gas is pretty much the same in principle, although you are waiting for the gas to heat up the grill bars, which is dependent on how close they are to the heat. The great thing about gas is you can control the heat directly by adjusting it up and down.

CLEANING TIPS

Unfortunately, one thing that most barbecues suffer from is neglect. I gave my Scouser mate Jamie Grainger-Smith a barbecue, and every time I went around I would say to him, 'Mate, you've got to give this thing a clean!' Did he listen? Then one day, halfway through cooking his famous jerked chicken, the thing exploded into a ball of flames. A grease fire!

Always give your barbecue a good clean after you've used it. While the barbecue is still warm, use a long-handled wire-bristle brush and paper towels to remove charred material and fat from the grill plates and bars, then wash the surfaces down with hot soapy water. Next, allow the barbecue to burn for 10–15 minutes to burn off any grease on the burners and grill tops. Change the absorbent material from the drip tray if it's excessively dirty.

When you come to use your barbecue again, give the grill bars and griddle plate another clean with a wire brush and paper towel. Importantly, prior to cooking you should allow your barbecue to burn very hot for a period (especially if it's gas) to burn off any debris or fat that may be left on the burners or hot rocks, as this may affect the flavour of your barbecue. I would also recommend a full strip down and a good deep clean at least once a year to prevent any serious fire accidents.

Kettle barbecues are a little easier to clean and maintain than gas. Most of the charcoal will burn to ash and will be caught in a tray underneath the bottom vents. The grill is easy to clean with a long-handled wire-bristle brush.

One thing both gas and kettle barbecues have in common is that neither of them like a lot of rain, so make sure you cover them when not in use.

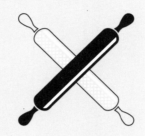

BREADS
and
BITES

DAMPER

FOCACCIA

BRUSCHETTA

MOZZARELLA WITH PEPPER AND BASIL BRUSCHETTA

MARINATED OLIVE AND MOZZARELLA BRUSCHETTA

FIG, MINT AND MOZZARELLA BRUSCHETTA

MARINATED FIRE-ROASTED PEPPER WITH ANCHOVY BRUSCHETTA

BRAZILIAN GARLIC BREAD

CHEESY GARLIC BREAD

PEPPERONI, OLIVE AND ANCHOVY PIZZA

POTATO AND BLUE CHEESE PIZZA

POLENTA

POLENTA WITH COPPA DI PARMA AND BLUE CHEESE

POLENTA WITH BUTTER, CHILLI AND CHEESE

QUESADILLAS

ZUCCHINI AND CHEESE QUESADILLAS

TORTILLAS

CHAPATTI

NAAN

ALOO GOBI PARATHAS

DAMPER

MAKES 1 LOAF

450 g organic self-raising flour,
plus extra for dusting

2 teaspoons sugar

1 heaped teaspoon salt

100 g lard or butter

150 ml milk, plus extra for brushing

150 ml water

butter, to serve

Damper is an Australian icon of bush cooking and backyard barbecuing, its roots going back to the swagmen of early European settlement. Usually cooked in the dying embers of an open fire or in a bush oven (a cast-iron pot), it's easily the simplest bread you could make on a barbecue.

The dough is made from the most basic ingredients that a traveller could carry: self-raising flour, lard or butter (more often lard, as it would keep better, and it produces the best results), salt, sugar, milk and water. As a kid, I always made damper when I went camping, but more often than not I was more interested in making it than eating it — with kids, it's always more about the journey than the destination.

The basic dough can be improved with the addition of herbs, olives or just about anything that takes your fancy. You can even make Damper doughnuts (page 240), stuffed with marshmallows.

Sieve the flour, sugar and salt together in a bowl. Using a fork, cut in the lard or butter until you have a texture that resembles breadcrumbs.

Mix in the milk and water, then lightly knead to form a dough.

Pat out onto a well-floured board or tray. Cut a cross into the dough, brush with milk and lightly flour the top. Place into a foil tray or baking dish.

Prepare your barbecue for indirect cooking on a medium heat (180°C if you have a thermometer). If you are cooking on a gas barbecue with a hood, turn the inner burners off and leave the outer ones on. For coal, build a fire on each side of the barbecue.

Cook the damper until golden, or until the bread sounds hollow when tapped.

Serve hot, with lots of butter.

FOCACCIA

I think focaccia is an ideal bread to cook on the barbecue, using either a kettle-style model or the hooded variety. The bread is generally not much more than a couple of centimetres thick, as it becomes a little too doughy otherwise. What's great about focaccia is that you can add a huge variety of toppings. Some suggestions are Marinated olives (page 69) or chopped rosemary and garlic.

Combine the warm water and semolina flour in a large bowl or mixing machine to make a porridge. The mixture should be room temperature.

Add the yeast and honey, using your hands to break up the yeast into the semolina. Allow the mixture to stand for 5–10 minutes, until bubbles start to appear.

Add the flour and salt, working the dough until it is smooth, soft and not too sticky. Dust the dough with a little flour, cover with a moist cloth and leave it to prove until doubled in size. This should take 30–45 minutes.

Tip the dough out onto a clean surface, knock it back and knead again. You may need to dust with a little flour to stop it from sticking.

Roll the dough out into a round, square or oval shape about 2 cm thick. Dust a baking tray with semolina flour, then lay the dough on top and press it out, if need be. Liberally oil the top of the bread and, using your fingertips as if you were playing the piano, press the surface of the bread so that it is pockmarked all over. Season well with salt flakes and a little pepper, and perhaps some fresh herbs and slivers of garlic.

If you are topping the bread with a garnish, simply use the pressing method to push it into the bread, along with a little olive oil. Allow the focaccia to prove for 40 minutes.

Prepare your barbecue for indirect cooking on a medium–hot heat. Bake the focaccia until the top is golden and the edges are crispy.

Allow the bread to cool slightly prior to serving. It's best served within 2 hours of baking.

MAKES 1 LOAF

350 ml warm water

250 g semolina flour, plus extra for kneading

15 g fresh yeast, or 7 g dried yeast

1 tablespoon honey

250 g pasta flour

1 teaspoon salt

extra virgin olive oil

sea salt flakes

freshly ground black pepper

chopped fresh herbs (optional)

garlic slivers (optional)

BRUSCHETTA

SERVES 8

12 slices sourdough bread, sliced 2 cm thick

2 garlic cloves, peeled

100 ml best-quality extra virgin olive oil,
or more to taste

good-quality crystal or rock salt

There is much discussion about what bruschetta really is or isn't. In its purest and simplest form, it is a grilled slice of bread that's simply rubbed with fresh garlic, drizzled with lashings of olive oil and seasoned with salt. A good bruschetta is a celebration of that true culinary champion, extra virgin olive oil.

The best bread to grill to make bruschetta is sourdough, slightly stale, as traditionally it was a way of using up older bread (the Italians are an economical people!) The bread can then be the vehicle for so many fantastic combinations of toppings.

Bruschetta is great to serve as snacks for a party, in a soup as croutons or under roast meat or stews to soak up the delicious gravy. It can even be turned into quite a substantial meal, depending on the topping.

Ensure that the barbecue is clean and dry of any oils. Place the slices of bread directly over the heat, allowing them to toast and take on the pattern from the grill. Turn the slices over and repeat the process on the other side.

Remove to a board or large plate and immediately rub the slices of bread once or twice with the garlic cloves, just to give a hint of garlic aroma.

Liberally drizzle with olive oil and season with salt.

Either enjoy the bruschetta as is, or top with anything you desire. You could try using olive bread as a variation.

MOZZARELLA
WITH
PEPPER AND BASIL
BRUSCHETTA

SERVES 8

1 quantity Bruschetta (previous page)

1 quantity Marinated fire-roasted peppers
with anchovies (page 52)

1 large buffalo mozzarella, sliced

torn basil leaves, to garnish

extra virgin olive oil

salt

freshly ground black pepper

Top each bruschetta with some roasted peppers
and a slice of mozzarella.

Garnish with a few basil leaves, add a drizzle of olive oil
and season with salt and pepper.

Arrange on platters and serve.

MARINATED
OLIVES
AND
MOZZARELLA
BRUSCHETTA

SERVES 8

1 quantity Bruschetta (previous page)

1 large buffalo mozzarella, sliced

Marinated olives (page 69)

Top each bruschetta with 2 slices of mozzarella and
sprinkle with 1 heaped tablespoon of the marinated olives.

Arrange on platters and serve.

FIG, MINT
AND
MOZZARELLA
BRUSCHETTA

SERVES 8

---

1 quantity Bruschetta (page 18)

4 ripe figs, sliced

juice of 1 lemon

extra virgin olive oil

salt

freshly ground black pepper

1 large buffalo mozzarella, sliced

chopped mint, to garnish

Only use the ripest figs you can find for this one. Dress the sliced figs with lemon juice, olive oil, salt and pepper.

Top each bruschetta with a layer of dressed figs and a slice of mozzarella.

Garnish with a little chopped mint and a drizzle of olive oil.

Arrange on platters and serve.

MARINATED
FIRE-ROASTED
PEPPER
WITH
ANCHOVY
BRUSCHETTA

SERVES 8

---

1 quantity Bruschetta (page 18)

1 quantity Marinated fire-roasted peppers with anchovies (page 52)

oregano or sweet marjoram leaves, to garnish

Top each bruschetta with the pepers and garnish with sweet marjoram or oregano.

Arrange on platters and serve.

BRAZILIAN
GARLIC
BREAD

This stuff is dangerous!

Using a stick blender, blend the egg yolks in a jug with the garlic and salt.

Slowly add the olive oil until you have a thick mayonnaise. Now slowly add the cream. Add half the dried oregano to the creamy mayo.

Cut incisions into the baguette, about three-quarters deep, and about one finger-space apart. Using a spoon, fill at least 1 tablespoon of the mayo between each slice.

Place a length of foil on the bench, then top with a similar length of baking paper.

Place the baguette in the middle. Fold the edges inwards once, then wrap the paper and foil up around the bread, leaving it a little loose and the top of the bread exposed.

Pour the remaining creamy mayo over the top of the bread. Sprinkle with the cheese and remaining oregano.

Cook on the resting rack of your barbecue at about 200°C for about 8–10 minutes or until the top of the bread is crispy and the cheese melted and golden brown. If you don't have a resting rack, bake it in the oven for the same time at the same temperature.

SERVES 4–6

3 egg yolks

5 garlic cloves

good pinch of salt

250 ml (1 cup) extra virgin olive oil

250 ml (1 cup) thick (heavy) cream

1 tablespoon dried oregano

1 long baguette

2 cups grated mature cheddar

CHEESY GARLIC BREAD

SERVES 4

1 long sourdough baguette

110 g mozzarella ball, chopped

200 g taleggio, chopped

200 g unsalted butter, soft

4 garlic cloves, finely chopped

2 teaspoons chopped flat-leaf parsley

1 teaspoon chopped sweet marjoram

salt

freshly ground black pepper

paprika (your choice of sweet or hot — I prefer sweet)

Garlic bread is always a winner at a barbecue. It's quick and easy, and hits the spot to help alleviate those hunger pains after you've been struggling to light the barbecue for the last hour. I find it's best to use a baguette, but you could just as easily use a ciabatta.

For me, this recipe is a throwback to Perth in the 1980s, which probably means the 1970s everywhere else in terms of cuisine! Garlic bread was huge at the time; every restaurant served it. Making garlic bread was my first job when I was an apprentice chef. The task was approached with great diligence and pride, because if your garlic bread was good, and you sold lots of it, you got the nod from the apprentices who'd come before you. There was also a lot of competition as to who made the best garlic bread. Try my recipe, and you be the judge.

Use a bread knife to cut diagonal slices along the loaf, cutting only three-quarters of the way into the bread with each slice.

Add the chopped cheeses to the butter, along with the garlic and herbs, and season with salt and pepper.

Spread the mix liberally between each slice of bread. Allow some of the butter to ooze from the top, as this will caramelise while cooking on the barbecue and taste wicked.

Wrap the bread in a doubled-over sheet of foil, leave the top exposed and sprinkle with paprika. Place on the barbecue with the lid on. If you have an uncovered barbecue, completely wrap the bread and just place it on the grill. Cook until crisp.

Serve while hot and the cheese is all gooey and delicious.

PEPPERONI,
OLIVE AND ANCHOVY
PIZZA

My all-time favourite pizza is probably 'The Pepperoni'. Hot and salty with olives and anchovies, it's perfect to wash down with cold beer!

Use the basic Focaccia recipe from page 17, mixing the dough as instructed. Leave it to prove for 30–45 minutes, until doubled in size, then make your pizza bases as instructed below.

You can basically top the pizza with whatever you like, but the principle is the same — don't over-top your pizza!

Preheat a pizza stone or tray on a barbecue over very high heat (250°C if you have a thermometer), or in the oven at 230°C.

Divide the dough into three balls. Roll each out on a separate sheet of lightly floured baking paper to about 2–3 mm thick (they don't have to be perfectly round).

Stack the bases on their paper, cover with a damp cloth and refrigerate until ready to cook — this stops them rising further.

Stir the garlic into the olive oil, then brush over the pizza bases.

Divide the passata among the bases, spreading it with a spoon to the edges.

Sprinkle the bases with the cheese, reserving about one-quarter for a final sprinkle.

Arrange the pepperoni slices in a circle around the pizzas, alternating with anchovies if you're using them.

Scatter with the olives, then the remaining cheese.

Transfer a pizza, still on its paper sheets, to the pizza stone or tray. Cover with the barbecue hood and cook for 5 minutes, or bake in the oven for 5–8 minutes, until the base is golden and crisp and the cheese melts.

Top with a third of the basil and season with pepper. Serve immediately and get the next pizza cooking!

**MAKES
3 PIZZAS**

1 quantity Focaccia (page 17)

2 garlic cloves, finely chopped

⅓ cup (80 ml) olive oil

500 ml (2 cups) tomato passata
(pureed tomatoes)

2 cups grated mozzarella

20 slices quality pepperoni

anchovy fillets (optional)

1 cup good-quality pitted black olives

½ cup chopped basil

freshly cracked black pepper

POTATO AND BLUE CHEESE PIZZA

MAKES
3 PIZZAS

1 quantity Focaccia (page 17)

2 large desiree potatoes, very thinly sliced
(a mandoline is ideal)

2 garlic cloves, finely chopped

⅓ cup (80 ml) olive oil

½ cup chopped basil

1 tablespoon finely chopped rosemary

150 g gorgonzola dolce, or other
soft blue cheese

150 g mozzarella or bocconcini

1 cup finely grated parmesan

1 bunch rocket, ends trimmed,
leaves washed

salt

freshly cracked black pepper

Preheat a pizza stone or tray on a barbecue over very high heat (250°C if you have a thermometer), or in the oven at 230°C.

Divide the dough into three balls. Roll each out on a separate sheet of lightly floured baking paper to about 2—3 mm thick (they don't have to be perfectly round).

Stack the bases on their paper, cover with a damp cloth and refrigerate until ready to cook — this will stop them rising further.

Rinse the potatoes in a colander and pat dry with a clean cloth.

Stir the garlic into 60 ml (¼ cup) of the olive oil, then brush over the pizza bases. Evenly scatter the bases with the potato slices, herbs and cheeses.

Transfer a pizza, still on its paper sheet, to the pizza stone or tray. Cover with the barbecue hood and cook for 5 minutes, or bake in the oven for 5—8 minutes, until the base is golden and crisp and the cheese melts.

Toss the rocket with the remaining olive oil. Season with salt and pepper and use for topping the pizzas.

Serve immediately and get the next pizza cooking!

Potato and blue cheese pizza (top);
Pepperoni, olive and anchovy pizza (bottom, page 25)

POLENTA

1.75 litres (7 cups) water

salt

300 g polenta

100 g unsalted butter

200 g parmesan, finely grated

freshly ground black pepper

The Spanish brought corn to Europe from the New World, and it is now a staple of many cuisines. I particularly love the way the Italians have embraced it. When I worked at London's River Café we served polenta every year, from late autumn into winter, while corn was in season. It's important to use a good-quality, ground polenta; I find the coarser, bramata style is best. Try to avoid the quick-cook stuff — it just doesn't have the flavour of the coarse, slow-cooking polenta.

The best part about cooking polenta is the fantastic crust at the bottom of the pan. We used to fight over the crust and add butter, parmesan and chopped chilli to it at the end. Gary, one of the Aussie chefs I worked with at the River Café, put me onto that little indulgence.

You will need to prepare the polenta in advance, as it has to set and then cool completely before it can be sliced and barbecued. Polenta can be served as a substitute for bread and it's also fantastic to give to your vegan mates to fill them up! It's a great accompaniment to grilled meats, especially pork, lamb or a great steak. Try the toppings I've suggested here, or simply top it with grilled field mushrooms and cheese.

Bring the water to the boil in a heavy-bottomed saucepan. Season well with salt.

Lower the heat to a simmer and slowly add the polenta in a continuous stream, stirring with a whisk until completely incorporated.

Bring the polenta to the boil. It should take on a thick quality, like slowly bubbling lava. Turn the heat down to low, so it bubbles only every so often, and cook for 30–40 minutes, until the grains are only just soft. Stir from time to time, to prevent the polenta from catching.

When cooked, stir in the butter, parmesan and pepper. Pour onto a wooden board or large plate and allow to set.

When completely cool, cut the polenta into strips or wedges and barbecue on a grill rack until crisp.

Check the fish after 40 minutes, when it should be just cooked. Remove from the barbecue and allow it to rest before serving.

POLENTA
WITH
COPPA DI PARMA
AND
BLUE CHEESE

Serve this polenta with a simple rocket salad.

SERVES 8

100 g gorgonzola dolce

1 tablespoon mascarpone

1 teaspoon chopped sweet marjoram or oregano

Coppa di Parma or prosciutto, sliced

1 quantity Polenta (previous page), grilled

juice of ½ lemon, or to taste

extra virgin olive oil

Place the gorgonzola, mascarpone and herbs in a small saucepan, and slowly cook until the cheese is just melted.

Place slices of Coppa di Parma on the grilled polenta, then dress with the cheese sauce, a squeeze of lemon juice and a drizzle of good quality olive oil.

POLENTA
WITH
BUTTER, CHILLI
AND
CHEESE

This one's an old favourite among chefs. There are no measurements — just use your intuition!

SERVES 8

1 quantity Polenta (previous page), grilled

unsalted butter, softened

parmesan, grated

red chillies, chopped

Simply spread the grilled polenta with butter — chefs tend to think the more butter, the better the taste! Sprinkle with parmesan and top with chopped chillies.

QUESADILLAS

Quesadillas are a great treat. Ideally, you should use raw dough to make them, although you can cheat and use flour tortillas from the supermarket and stuff them with your filling of choice. The great thing about making your own dough is that you can flavour it with chillies, cheese or fresh herbs.

Quesadillas are perfect for stuffing with Refried beans (page 51).

MAKES 10–12

300 g masa harina (tortilla flour)

50 g plain flour

½ teaspoon baking powder

60 ml (¼ cup) corn oil or vegetable oil

1 large egg, beaten

175 ml milk

Place the dry ingredients in a large bowl and combine thoroughly.

Stir in the oil, egg and enough milk to make a firm dough.

Form into balls and press out into large circles.

Place your filling in the middle of one half of each quesadilla, then fold over. Seal the edges by pressing them together, wetting the edges slightly if necessary to get them to stick.

Prepare your barbecue for cooking on a medium heat. Lightly oil the hotplate of your barbecue or griddle pan and cook the quesadillas for 2–3 minutes on each side.

ZUCCHINI AND CHEESE QUESADILLAS

MAKES 10–12

1 zucchini (courgette), grated

1 cup grated cheddar

1 cup grated mozzarella

2 tablespoons chopped basil

salt

freshly ground black pepper

1 quantity Quesadilla dough (previous page)

Combine the zucchini and cheeses. Add the basil, salt and pepper. Place the cheese mix inside the quesadillas and seal.

Cook as described in the Quesadillas recipe.

TORTILLAS

275 g masa harina (tortilla flour)
½ teaspoon salt
300 ml lukewarm water

Tortilla means 'little cake' in Spanish, and is not to be confused with the Spanish omelette of the same name. Tortillas are generally made using a ground corn flour called masa harina, which means 'dough flour'.

Tortillas are fundamental to Mexican cuisine, forming the basis of many dishes. They are also easy to make and very economical. All you need is a tortilla press, and off you go! Get them mastered and you can be making tacos, tostadas and chilaquiles. You can use a number of recipes in this book to fill the very versatile tortilla. Try the Mexican suckling pig tortillas (page 148), or you could even use a marinated skirt steak (see the Aussie steak sandwich for an example, on page 142).

Combine the masa harina and salt in a large bowl.

Add 250 ml (1 cup) of the water and mix until it forms a dough. Test the dough in your press by placing a small ball of dough between two sheets of plastic bag and closing the press. If the dough is too dry, it will crumble; if it is too wet, it will stick to the plastic.

If the dough is too wet, add more masa; if it's too dry, add a little water. It's hard to say how much water will be required as humidity affects the dough, as does the age of the flour. Fresh masa needs less water than older flour.

If the dough is correct, form balls about 4 cm in diameter. Place the balls, one at a time, between two sheets of plastic bag and press to flatten into a circle about 10 cm wide. Remove the top plastic sheet, then lift and turn the tortilla over onto your palm and peel away the other sheet of plastic.

Prepare your barbecue for cooking on a medium heat. Place the tortillas on the grill top, or on a heavy skillet if using a kettle or open coal fire. Cook for 1 minute, until the edges curl upwards, then flip and cook for another minute. The tortillas should be lightly speckled; the first side cooked is the top.

Eat the tortillas straight away, or keep them warm by wrapping them in a cloth and placing them inside a heavy warm pot.

CHAPATTI

A chapatti is a very simple, firm flour dough that's rolled flat and then cooked on a barbecue hotplate. I like to use my tortilla press when I'm making chapattis — not only is it easy, you also get a great random shape. All you have to do is place a nice portion of dough in the centre of the press and pull down on the handle. Chapattis are best served hot, and they go particularly well with satay skewers or tandoori dishes.

The hand is used more frequently than knives and forks in India, and the chapatti is handy to scoop up all those lovely juices. The addition of a few whole spices like fennel or cumin can make a subtle but great addition to the basic recipe.

Combine the salt and flour, and add enough water to form a semi-hard dough. Wrap in plastic wrap and rest for 20 minutes.

Divide the dough into 8–10 balls, then either press in a tortilla press or roll out on a clean surface using a rolling pin. You shouldn't need extra flour if the dough is firm enough.

Prepare your barbecue for cooking on a medium heat. Oil the hotplate and cook the chapattis for just a few minutes, turning them often.

Serve hot.

MAKES 8–10

1 teaspoon salt
250 g wholemeal atta flour
50 ml sunflower oil

NAAN

525 g wholemeal atta flour or strong plain flour,
plus extra for dusting

pinch of salt

10 g fresh yeast, or 5 g dried yeast

1 teaspoon caster sugar

125 ml (½ cup) warm water

1 egg, beaten

3 tablespoons biodynamic yoghurt

melted clarified butter, to serve

You'll find this type of bread across the whole of Asia. The most famous variety is the Indian incarnation, cooked in the terracotta tandoor ovens of the Punjab. Naans are simple to make, and they are a great alternative to serving everyday breads at a barbecue. They come either plain or packed with a variety of fillings like dried fruit and coconut.

You could add chopped garlic to the clarified butter in this recipe if you'd like a more flavoursome naan. This bread is ideal to serve with Whole pumpkin biryani (page 58) or Barbecued pepper chicken curry (page 172).

Combine the flour and salt, and mix well.

Mix the yeast and sugar with the warm water and allow to stand for 5–10 minutes, until the mixture starts to foam. Add the egg and yoghurt.

Combine the yeast mixture with the flour and knead until you have a smooth, soft dough. Cover with a wet cloth, place in a warm spot and leave it to prove until doubled in size.

Once the dough has proved, knock it back and allow it to prove again until it has doubled in size once again.

Divide the dough into equal-sized balls. Pat them out on a floured surface to a roughly round or oval shape, about 5 mm thick. Do not roll them out with a rolling pin.

Cook the naan straight on the grill racks of a medium–hot kettle barbecue with the lid on. You could also cook them directly on a dry hotplate with the hood down.

Brush the cooked naan with clarified butter and serve while hot.

ALOO GOBI
PARATHAS

My mate Serif's mum comes from India, and she's the best cook. Serif's house was our favourite meeting place when I was growing up: we would hang out in his old man's shed, fixing our bikes trying to get Serif's go-cart to work. His mum always had a huge pot of curry on the stove and we would just help ourselves, but the highlight would be when she had her extended family over. If you were lucky enough to rock up when that was happening you were in for a treat, because that's when parathas were made — awesome roti breads stuffed with meat, vegetables and spices.

These parathas are great by themselves or with a curry, but you don't need to save them for when you're putting on an Indian-style meal. They should be cooked whenever you have a barbecue! The vegos will love them, especially served with spiced yoghurt (page 160) or Spiced red bean salad (page 88).

To make the dough, combine the flour and salt. Mix in the oil and add enough water to form a soft but not sticky dough. Wrap in plastic wrap and rest for 20 minutes.

Boil the potatoes in their skins in salted water. Meanwhile, in another saucepan, cook the cauliflower in salted water until soft.

Once the potatoes are cooked, peel and mash them. Drain the cauliflower, then crush it and mix it with the potatoes.

Add the remaining ingredients, apart from the oil for frying. When combined, season with salt.

To make the parathas, take a portion of the roti dough and flatten it in your palm. Add a spoonful of the potato and cauliflower mixture, then roll the dough into a ball. Using a rolling pin, flatten the ball to around 1 cm thick.

Prepare your barbecue for cooking on a medium heat. Lightly oil the hotplate and cook the parathas until both sides are golden and cooked through.

Serve straight away.

MAKES 4

250 g plain flour

pinch of salt

50 ml sunflower oil

FILLING

300 g potatoes

salt

200 g cauliflower

2 tablespoons chopped coriander leaves

2 teaspoons garlic paste

2 teaspoons ginger paste

75 g onion, finely chopped

½ green chilli, chopped

1 teaspoon ground turmeric

1 teaspoon chilli powder

juice of 1 lime

sunflower oil, for frying

VEGETABLES
and
SALADS

GRILLED HALOUMI

GRILLED VERDURE MISTE

ROBATAYAKI VEGETABLES

BABA GHANOUSH

COAL-BAKED ARTICHOKES

ARTICHOKES WITH LEMON, HONEY, THYME AND ALMOND DRESSING

BAKED BEANS

REFRIED BEANS

FIRE-ROASTED PEPPERS

MARINATED FIRE-ROASTED PEPPERS WITH ANCHOVIES

BAKED SWEET POTATOES WITH SPECK, CLOVES AND MAPLE SYRUP

BAKED SWEET POTATOES WITH GREEN CHILLI AND LEMON OIL

CARIBBEAN RICE AND PEAS

WHOLE PUMPKIN BIRYANI

BARBECUED CORN WITH BACON AND CHILLI BUTTER

RUSTIC SPANISH POTATOES

GRILLED TOMATOES AND COTTAGE CHEESE

BALSAMIC ROSEMARY ONIONS

BROCCOLI AND SPINACH 'COUSCOUS'

SPICED POTATO AND CHICKPEA DOSA

MARINATED OLIVES

BARBECUED AVOCADO WITH HERB LABNEH SALAD

PANZANELLA

COLESLAW

CARROT SALAD

PINEAPPLE, CUCUMBER AND CHILLI SALAD

VIETNAMESE RICE NOODLE SALAD

STUFFED GEM SQUASH

KIMCHI

SUGAR LOAF CABBAGE CORIANDER AND MINT SALAD

CRUNCHY CUCUMBER MINT AND CHILLI SALAD

SOM TAM: GREEN PAPAYA SALAD

SHAVED FENNEL AND CELERY SALAD

TABOULEH

SPICED RED BEAN SALAD

GRILLED
HALOUMI

SERVES 6

200 g good-quality haloumi (Greek if possible)

1 tablespoon olive oil

2 tablespoons chopped mint

juice of 1 lemon

I've only been to one Greek island, Mykonos, but I've been to many good Greek restaurants in Sydney, London and Melbourne, which has the third-largest Greek population outside Greece. The best Greek experience I've ever had was when I was in Wellington, New Zealand. We went to the house of a Greek Cypriot family who put on a barbecue like nothing you have ever seen. Their son was a cheesemaker whose speciality was an authentic Cypriot haloumi cheese flecked with fresh mint, a traditional addition.

There is only one way to eat haloumi, and that is simply grilled on a hotplate and served with fresh lemon and mint. It's a great way to get the hordes' appetites started and kept at bay while you get on with the main show.

Prepare your barbecue hotplate or griddle pan for cooking over a medium–high heat.

Cut the haloumi into flattish rectangles, about a finger thick.

Pour the oil onto the hot griddle or barbecue hotplate. Cook the haloumi until golden and crispy on both sides.

Remove to a plate and scatter with chopped mint and a squeeze of lemon juice.

Serve hot.

GRILLED VERDURE MISTE

So, you've gone all out with your pit of fire, and you've slow-cooked your pork shoulder or hunk of beef. It's an orgy of carnivorous delights and now your mates have turned up, and, surprise, surprise, one of them has brought a vegan! No drama you say, and really there shouldn't be, not when you can impress everyone with this great combination of barbecued vegies.

It's hard to give exact volumes for this recipe, as it's more or less of what you like, but the general process is what is important. Firstly, build your fire or adjust your gas so that you have a hot side and a cooler side of the barbecue. Secondly, always start with the vegetables that will take the longest to cook. Adding a spray of water to the vegetables while they're cooking speeds the process along, as the water evaporates on the barbecue, creating steam. I never add oil because it burns by the time the vegies are cooked, giving them an unpleasant taste.

Serve garnished with freshly cut herbs or maybe some balsamic vinegar or feta.

If you are using butternut pumpkin, cut it in half, then into wedges about as thick as your finger. If you are using a round pumpkin, cut it into crescents, again about as thick as your finger. Toss the pumpkin with a little water and salt and pepper.

Cut the other vegetables into pieces that are sympathetic to their natural shapes, relative to their size and the other vegetables you are cooking. Toss with a little water and salt and pepper.

Place the vegetables on the hottest part of the barbecue to char them with the marks of the grill, then move them to the lower heat. Cook until just tender, as the residual heat will continue to steam and soften the vegetables once they are removed from the heat.

Transfer the vegetables to a large bowl as they cook, taking care to mix the different varieties together.

To make the dressing, place the garlic in a mortar and pound with a little salt and the herbs to form a paste. Add vinegar and olive oil to make a vinaigrette, then toss with the grilled vegetables.

Season with salt and pepper, then serve.

SERVES 4

pumpkin (squash), such as butternut, peeled

salt

freshly ground black pepper

baby leeks

fennel

red onions

finger eggplant (aubergine)

zucchini (courgette)

kipfler (fingerling) or pink fir apple potatoes

DRESSING

2 garlic cloves, peeled

salt

2 tablespoons chopped herbs
(basil, marjoram or dried wild oregano)

2 tablespoons white wine vinegar

60 ml (¼ cup) extra virgin olive oil

freshly ground black pepper

ROBATAYAKI
VEGETABLES

Robatayaki is a style of cooking seafood and vegetables, and less frequently meat and poultry, over a charcoal grill. Traditionally, robatayakis were inns or meeting places that had an open fire (robata) in the middle of the room, the centre of activity. As with Japanese food in general, presentation is of major importance, so most robatayaki dishes are small morsels and are simply presented on bamboo skewers. Common ingredients include asparagus, mushrooms, tofu and finger eggplants (aubergines). They're generally seasoned with kecap manis or miso sauce.

SERVES 4

24 thick asparagus spears

kecap manis

1 teaspoon sesame seeds

Soak 8 bamboo skewers for 1 hour in some water.

Trim the asparagus to 12 cm lengths, making sure they are perfectly even and the base of each stem is cut on a slight angle.

Thread three pieces of asparagus onto a skewer. Make sure they're evenly spaced and threaded halfway along the asparagus. Repeat with the remaining asparagus, allowing two skewers per person.

Place on the grill and cook for 2 minutes on each side.

Remove to a plate, drizzle with kecap manis and sprinkle with a few sesame seeds. Serve with Asian herbs.

MISO
EGGPLANT

SERVES 6

12 finger eggplants (aubergines), halved lengthwise

100 g Miso marinade (page 268)

Soak 12 bamboo skewers for 1 hour in some water.

Carefully cut a crisscross pattern into the flesh of the eggplants. Thread 2 eggplant halves onto each skewer. Repeat with the remaining eggplants, allowing 2 skewers per person.

Brush the eggplants with half the marinade and allow to infuse for 20 minutes.

Place the eggplants flesh side down on a hot grill for 1–2 minutes. Turn them over and cook for a further 5 minutes, or until soft.

Remove the eggplants to plates and brush with a little more miso marinade.

BABA
GHANOUSH

Eggplants (aubergines) are perfect for cooking on the barbecue, either grilled or charred in the fire. For this recipe, they are cooked whole until they are soft and take on an incredible smoky flavour. Baba ghanoush is great as a dip to share while the main meal is cooking, or as an accompaniment with kofte, shish or simply grilled lamb, chicken, salmon or mackerel.

Place the eggplants directly in the fire or on the grill and allow to cook, turning, until very soft and charred all over. They will look burnt. Remove from the fire and allow to cool.

Peel away the burnt outer skin with a small, sharp knife or cut in half and scoop out the flesh. Place the flesh in a sieve or colander to drain, as the eggplants will have a lot of moisture in them.

Using a whisk, fork or blender, break down the eggplant to a pulp.

Season with salt and pepper, then add tahini and chopped garlic. Add the lemon juice and olive oil, and combine.

Check the seasoning and texture. The baba ghanoush should be creamy.

Serve sprinkled with the toasted cumin seeds.

SERVES 4

2 large eggplants (aubergines)

salt

freshly ground black pepper

1 large tablespoon tahini

2 garlic cloves, chopped

juice of 2 lemons

2 tablespoons olive oil

1 teaspoon toasted cumin seeds

COAL-BAKED
ARTICHOKES

SERVES 4

4 large globe artichokes, or 8 violet
or spiny artichokes

I love artichokes and the endless ways of preparing them. The method I saw demonstrated when I attended a cooking school in a small Sicilian village called Regaleali is truly the best and most simple.

A fire in a large open pit is allowed to burn down to a mass of smouldering coals, into which whole artichokes are pushed. It means that you don't end up with bitter, stained fingers from cleaning the artichokes first. Once they are cooked, you can do what you like with them — preserve them in oil, make salads with them or serve them in the dressing described on page 49.

There are many varieties of artichokes, but I recommend that you use the larger globe or smaller violet or spiny ones. Choose artichokes that are firm and have a tightly closed flower, as these will have a smaller percentage of the furry choke at the centre.

Build a good hot coal base and allow it to burn down to an even white bed of ashen coals. The coals should be deep enough to cover three-quarters of each artichoke.

Cut the stem of each artichoke to about 2 cm from the base. Use a serrated knife to trim the top by around 2 cm.

Push the artichokes into the coals using a long pair of tongs, to avoid burning yourself. Place the artichokes as close together as possible and push the coals up and around them.

Allow the artichokes to cook until they are tender to the prick of a knife or skewer.

Remove to a large bowl and allow them to cool so you can handle them.

Once cool, use a small knife to peel off the outer leaves, one at a time, until you reach the first of the tender inside leaves. Trim the stem by scraping it with the knife. Cut the artichokes in half and remove all the furry choke fibres.

ARTICHOKES
WITH LEMON, HONEY, THYME AND ALMOND
DRESSING

We used to cook this recipe at the River Café in London, and it's a great combination. Make sure you use a good-quality honey.

While you are waiting for the artichokes to cool, pound the garlic, thyme and a little salt in a mortar to a paste.

Add the honey and lemon juice and zest, and combine well. Mix in the olive oil.

Peel and cut the artichokes into quarters. While they are still warm, toss with the dressing and season with salt and pepper to taste.

Serve sprinkled with the almonds.

SERVES 4

1 quantity Coal-baked artichokes (page 46)

1 garlic clove, peeled

1 tablespoon thyme

salt

1 tablespoon honey

zest and juice of 1 lemon

100 ml olive oil

freshly cracked black pepper

½ cup toasted flaked almonds

BAKED
BEANS

SERVES 8

250 g dried or 500 g freshly podded cannellini or borlotti beans

1 teaspoon bicarbonate of soda (if using dried beans)

400 g can chopped or pureed roma (plum) tomatoes

1 rosemary sprig

small bunch sage

2 celery stalks

5 garlic cloves, peeled

1 dried chilli or chipotle chilli

salt

freshly ground black pepper

extra virgin olive oil

juice of 1 lemon

Legumes such as borlotti, cannellini and kidney beans are a fantastic accompaniment to a barbecue. Fresh legumes are generally available during spring and early summer, which means they are at their best when you want to crank up the barbecue. You can also use dried beans, which you can buy at most supermarkets. If you like your beans to have a smoky flavour, try using a chipotle (a dried smoked jalapeño) instead of a dried chilli. Any leftovers can be used to make Refried beans (next page) for an accompaniment to Mexican-style dishes.

I like to use Qbags (aluminium foil bags) to cook the beans, as there is less messing about, but if you don't have them you can use an enamel or metal roasting dish instead.

If you're using dried beans, soak them overnight in plenty of cold water and add 1 teaspoon of bicarbonate of soda (this helps to soften the skins). If you're using fresh beans, just wash and drain them.

Prepare your barbecue for cooking over a medium heat.

Combine the beans and tomatoes in a bowl. Transfer to a roasting dish or Qbags.

Sandwich the rosemary and sage between the two celery stalks and tie together to stop the herbs mixing in with the beans when cooking. Put this in with the beans, along with the garlic and chilli. Top with water — 250 ml (1 cup) if using fresh beans, 500 ml (2 cups) if using dried.

Either seal the bags with two firm folds, or wrap the dish with foil and seal well.

Place on the barbecue hotplate and cook for 40 minutes, until the beans are soft and most of the liquid has been absorbed.

When cooked, open the bags or remove the foil and discard the celery and herbs and dried chilli. Stir the beans and mash a few with the back of a spoon.

Transfer to a serving bowl, season with salt and pepper, and finish with a splash of extra virgin olive oil and lemon juice.

REFRIED
BEANS

The original name for these beans, frijoles refrito, doesn't mean that the beans are fried twice. They're simply baked or boiled and then fried with lard or oil. Lard is the better of the two because of its richer flavour, but for those with an aversion to lard, olive oil is fine. I generally use the leftovers from my Baked beans (previous page). It's important that the beans are relatively free of liquid.

Refried beans are great with Tortillas (page 36) or Quesadillas (page 31), or as a dip served with tortilla chips. They can also accompany grilled meat or chicken. Think of this dish as Mexican mash!

Prepare your barbecue for cooking over a medium heat.

Heat some lard or oil on the barbecue hotplate and add a couple of large spoonfuls of beans. Mash with a scraper and repeat the process until all the beans are cooked, adding a little lard or oil as you go.

Remove the mash to a serving dish.

To serve, sprinkle with the cheese and season with salt and pepper.

SERVES 4

100 g lard, or 100 ml olive oil
½ quantity Baked beans (previous page)
100 g grated cheddar
salt
freshly ground black pepper

FIRE-ROASTED PEPPERS

Just about every Italian I have spoken to about barbecuing capsicums or peppers says that putting them directly into the fire to cook gives them a flavour that's so sublime, no gas grill can match it. This method is great, as the direct contact with the coals speeds the process along.

I once worked with the Sicilian director Carmelo Musca. Gesticulating passionately, he described the way his mother prepared sweet peppers. With my imagination stimulated, I could smell the sweet, burnt skin blistering to reveal the lush flesh impregnated with the soul of the fire.

These peppers work a treat on Bruschetta (page 18). It's best to use long, pointed peppers. The great thing about using a plastic bag when preparing them is that you can leave all the charred and discarded material inside the bag, which you can then tie up and dispose of without any mess.

SERVES 6

6 firm-fleshed peppers

Build a good hot coal base and allow it to burn down to an even white bed of ashen coals.

Place the peppers around the edge of the fire, and use long-handled tongs to turn them so their skin is charred evenly on all sides. When the peppers are blackened all over, either put them in a stainless-steel bowl and cover with cling wrap or put them in a plastic bag and tie to seal. Allow the peppers to cool sufficiently so you can handle them.

Prepare the peppers by pushing the charred skin away from the flesh, removing the stalk and slitting the peppers to remove the seeds.

MARINATED FIRE-ROASTED PEPPERS WITH ANCHOVIES

SERVES 6

salt
freshly ground black pepper
extra virgin olive oil
2 teaspoons chopped sweet marjoram or basil
1 quantity Fire-roasted peppers (page 52)
12 anchovy fillets
1 garlic clove, sliced

Sprinkle a plate with salt and pepper, a little olive oil and half the herbs. Place the peppers on the platter.

Arrange the anchovies, remaining herbs and garlic over the top of the peppers.

To serve, season with pepper and drizzle once again with olive oil.

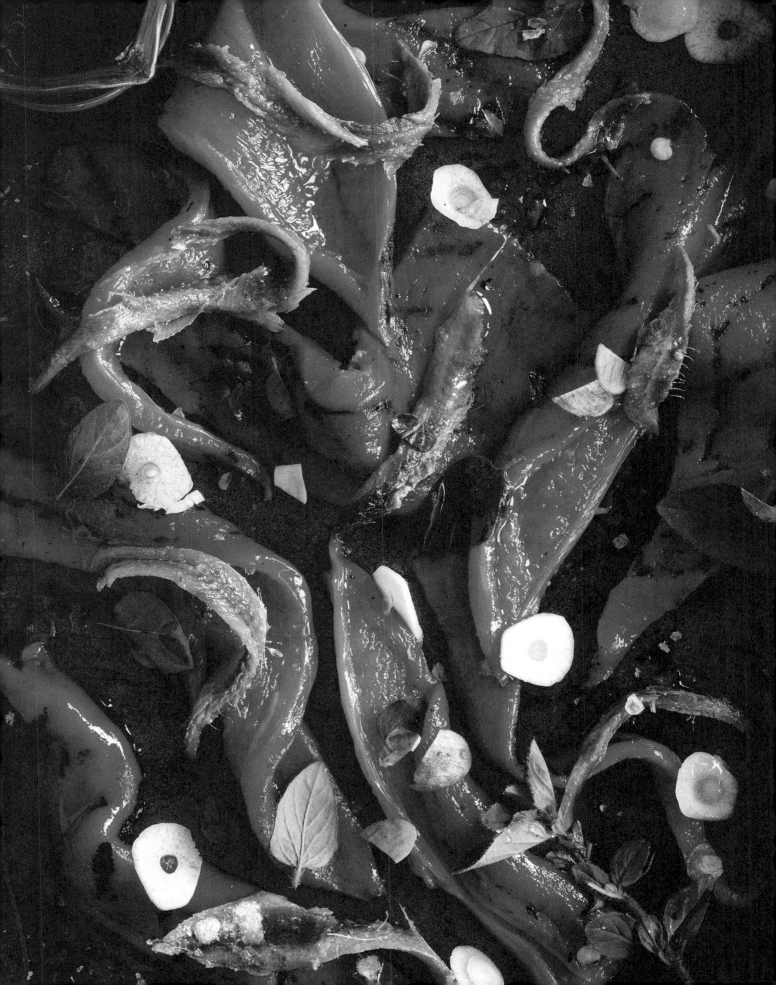

BAKED
SWEET POTATOES
WITH SPECK, CLOVES
AND MAPLE SYRUP

Sweet potatoes have been cultivated as a source of food for thousands of years. New Zealand/Aotearoa's Māori have a long history of cultivating kumara, though compared to the varieties we eat today they tended to be small — generally no bigger than a finger. The sweet potato evolved from an American vegetable, and over time red, gold and orange potatoes have been cultivated. It's a very nutritious vegetable, high in vitamins A and C.

There are endless ways to prepare sweet potatoes, but, just like potatoes baked in their skins, you can't beat the flavour when they're simply prepared. Here are two of my favourite ways to cook sweet potatoes on the barbecue.

Wrap each sweet potato in two pieces of speck or bacon. Use cloves to secure the bacon.

Firmly wrap each sweet potato in two sheets of foil.

Prepare your barbecue for cooking over a medium heat. If using charcoal, insert the sweet potatoes along the edge of the coals; if using gas, place them over the gas burners on the grilling bars.

Cook the sweet potatoes until they are quite soft. Depending on the size of the vegetables, this may take 30 minutes.

When cooked, discard the foil, slit the sweet potatoes open with a sharp knife and place on a serving plate.

Drizzle with maple syrup and season with salt and pepper. Serve straight away.

SERVES 4

4 sweet potatoes, washed and dried

8 strips of speck or smoked streaky bacon

4 cloves

2 tablespoons maple syrup

salt

freshly cracked black pepper

BAKED
SWEET POTATOES
WITH GREEN CHILLI
AND
LEMON OIL

SERVES 4

4 sweet potatoes, washed and dried

2 green chillies, seeded and finely chopped

zest of 1 lemon

2 tablespoons extra virgin olive oil

salt

Firmly wrap each sweet potato in two sheets of foil.

Prepare your barbecue for cooking over a medium heat. If using charcoal, insert the sweet potatoes along the edge of the coals; if using gas, place them over the gas burners on the grilling bars.

Cook the sweet potatoes until they are quite soft. The cooking time will depend on the size of the vegetables, and may take about 30 minutes.

When cooked, discard the foil, slit the sweet potatoes open with a sharp knife and place on a serving plate.

Combine the chillies with the lemon zest and olive oil.

To serve, dress the sweet potatoes with the chilli mixture and season with salt.

CARIBBEAN RICE AND BEANS

This classic Caribbean dish is perfect served with the hot, aromatic flavours of Jerked chicken (page 164) or Carribean jerked red fish (page 115). It's sometimes known as 'dirty rice', probably because of the effect of the beans on the rice, but in no way does it reflect its wonderful flavour.

It's an easy dish to prepare and can be cooked outside on the side burner of the barbecue or indoors on the stove.

Place the beans, water, coconut cream, thyme, chilli and spring onions in a saucepan, and season to taste. Bring to the boil.

Add the rinsed rice and butter, and boil for 2–3 minutes. Lower the heat to a simmer, cover with a lid and cook for 35 minutes.

Once cooked, sprinkle with the coriander and spring onions and serve.

SERVES 4

225 g can black-eye beans

700 ml water

400 ml can coconut cream

1 teaspoon chopped thyme leaves

1 teaspoon Scotch bonnet chilli (or other hot red chilli), seeded and chopped

2 spring onions, chopped

salt

freshly ground black pepper

450 g basmati rice, washed 3 times

25 g butter

¼ cup chopped coriander leaves and spring onions to serve

WHOLE
PUMPKIN
BIRYANI

SERVES 8

100 g basmati rice

1 large (1.5–2 kg) butternut pumpkin (squash)

2 tablespoons tinned chopped tomatoes

1 tablespoon chopped mint

1 tablespoon coriander leaves

pinch of saffron threads

1 teaspoon garam masala

MARINADE

10 g garlic, peeled

10 g fresh ginger, peeled

2 red chillies

sunflower oil

4 tablespoons yoghurt

juice of 1 lemon

1 teaspoon ground turmeric

salt, to taste

SPICE MIX

2 tablespoons vegetable oil

1 onion, sliced

3 cardamom pods, crushed

¼ teaspoon ground cinnamon

2 cloves

1 bay leaf

The first time I ate a whole stuffed pumpkin (squash) was when I was staying in Plettenbergbaai in South Africa, a place that reminded me of Byron Bay. While I was there I had the most amazing braai (barbecue) I have ever experienced.

For this recipe I have taken another influence, Indian, which is strong in South Africa, and combined it with pumpkin. Vegetable biryanis are more common than meat ones, so it makes sense really. It takes a little preparation, but if you're going on a picnic you could prepare this and wrap it up to take along, as it travels so well.

Wash and drain the rice until the water runs clear, then boil until two-thirds cooked. Drain and refresh.

To make the marinade, puree the garlic, ginger and chillies with a little sunflower oil to help loosen the mix. Combine with the remaining marinade ingredients.

Halve the butternut pumpkin, remove the seeds and scoop out the flesh to create a large cavity in each half. Chop the scooped-out pumpkin into dice and add half the dice to the marinade. Keep the remaining pumpkin dice for soup or another use.

To make the spice mix, heat the oil in a heavy-bottomed frying pan or on the hotplate and cook the onion. Add the remaining spice mix ingredients, and fry until slightly golden. Remove from the heat and set aside.

Combine the marinated pumpkin with the tinned tomatoes.

Spoon the pumpkin mixture into the two pumpkin halves, then add alternate layers of cooked rice, spice mix, chopped mint and coriander leaves.

Sprinkle saffron over the top of each pumpkin half then sandwich the two halves together. Wrap tightly in three or four layers of foil and place in the coals or on the edge of the barbecue to cook for 1½ hours.

To serve, open the two halves and sprinkle with the garam masala.

BARBECUED CORN WITH BACON AND CHILLI BUTTER

Corn on the cob is one of those things that's enjoyed by the whole family. I love that it's such a simple thing to cook and that eating it is so hands-on. If you prefer not to use chilli in the butter, use parmesan or anything you fancy.

I've often come across corn recipes like this one while researching American barbecuing techniques. Here, I have combined the flavours with a barbecued corn dish I had in New York at a funky Cuban diner. The highlight that day was not the corn but that I saw Meg White from the White Stripes there having lunch. The lime-chilli butter they served with the corn was great though.

Prepare your barbecue for cooking over a medium heat.

Prepare the corn by pulling back the outer husks and removing all the strands of fibre, but without removing the husks.

Place a bacon rasher on either side of each cob and season with pepper. Wrap the corn cobs back in their husks and secure with string at the top and bottom.

Cook the corn cobs for 30 minutes, continually turning them to prevent the husks burning.

Meanwhile, make the chilli butter by combining the butter, chilli and lime zest, and seasoning with salt and pepper.

When the corn is cooked, remove to a serving dish, untie the string and peel back the husks. Serve with a dollop of chilli butter.

SERVES 4

4 corn cobs, in their husks
8 rashers smoked streaky bacon
freshly ground black pepper

CHILLI BUTTER

100 g unsalted butter, softened
1 red chilli, chopped
zest of 1 lime
salt
freshly ground black pepper

RUSTIC SPANISH POTATOES

SERVES 6

500 g new potatoes, washed

2 garlic cloves, chopped

12 vine-ripened cherry tomatoes, crushed

1 red pepper, cut into large dice

salt

freshly ground black pepper

100 ml olive oil

175 ml white wine

pinch of saffron threads

1 tablespoon chopped flat-leaf parsley

Potatoes have been a staple part of Western diets for centuries, thanks to the Spanish bringing them to Europe along with their plunder from the Americas. The potato took a while to take off, as it was seen as a food for the underclasses, and also because of its association with poison, as it is a member of the deadly nightshade family.

Here's a rustic Spanish-style potato dish I thought I'd include. It's great with meat and fish, and is served warm. I use Qbags (aluminium foil bags) to do mine on the barbecue, but you could also use a saucepan.

Prepare your barbecue for cooking over a medium heat.

Cut the potatoes so they are all an equal size.

If you are using a saucepan, place the potatoes and garlic in a bowl. Put the tomatoes and red pepper in a separate bowl and season with salt and pepper. Heat the oil, then add the potatoes and garlic and cook until the outer edges begin to go translucent. Add the tomatoes and red pepper, and fry for 1 minute. Add the wine and saffron, and allow to gently simmer for 40 minutes, until the potatoes are tender, the tomatoes have broken down and the peppers are soft. When cooked, remove from the heat and allow to stand.

If you are using a Qbag, combine the ingredients in a bowl and season with salt and pepper. Place the mixture in the bag (or bags), seal and place on the barbecue to cook for about 40 minutes. Shake the bag from time to time. When cooked, remove from the heat and allow to stand.

Check the seasoning and serve the potatoes topped with chopped parsley.

GRILLED TOMATOES
AND
COTTAGE CHEESE

You can't have a barbecue without tomatoes showing up in some form or other, whether in a straight salad or in tasty sauces and glazes.

The big trend nowadays is for 'heirloom' varieties, the types of tomatoes that used to be grown but which for commercial reasons have dropped by the wayside — either because of the small volumes they produced or because they don't travel well to market.

When we filmed an episode of Surfing the Menu on the Mornington Peninsula in Victoria, we visited a garden called Heronswood that specialises in growing and sourcing heirloom plants. You can buy an amazing number of tomato varieties online and it's worth having a go, because there is nothing like the flavour of homegrown tomatoes.

My granddad always said that you can't beat an English tomato, and this recipe is inspired by the wonderful tomatoes I get from the Isle of Wight. Serve this dish with spicy Peri-peri chicken (page 167).

Prepare your barbecue for cooking over a high heat.

Cut the tomatoes in half, in irregular shapes. Season with a little salt, pour on a little olive oil and add the rosemary.

Combine the cottage cheese with the remaining olive oil, garlic, salt, pepper and half the chopped soft herbs.

Place the tomatoes cut side down on a very hot barbecue grill and cook until charred.

When cooked, remove to a serving plate. Scatter over the cottage cheese mixture and season.

To serve, garnish with the remaining fresh herbs.

SERVES 6

1 kg mixed-variety tomatoes, washed

salt

60 ml (¼ cup) extra virgin olive oil

1 tablespoon chopped rosemary

250 g cottage cheese

1 garlic clove, chopped

freshly cracked black pepper

fresh herbs (such as flat-leaf parsley, mint, oregano), chopped

BALSAMIC
ROSEMARY
ONIONS

SERVES 6

6 onions
120 ml balsamic vinegar
salt
freshly ground black pepper
300 g butter, cut into 12 cubes
6 rosemary sprigs

A barbecue just doesn't feel like a barbecue unless there are onions. This recipe is a great way to serve them as an accompaniment to whole joints of beef or lamb cooked on the barbecue. I like to use a charcoal fire for this one — which isn't to say that cooking the onions over gas won't be as awesome! Make sure the onions you choose have firm, intact and clean skins.

The flavours in this recipe are akin to sweet and sour: you have the wonderful sweetness of the slow-cooked onion, and the woody, sweet and sharp flavour of the balsamic. Try cooking them in a conventional oven as well, I would recommend cooking them for 45 minutes at about 160°C.

Prepare your barbecue for cooking over a medium heat.

Cut a deep cross into the top of each onion, cutting one-third of the way into each one.

Force your thumb into the incision and prise it open a little. Place 1–2 teaspoons of the vinegar inside, then season with salt and pepper. Press a cube of butter into each onion, followed by a sprig of rosemary.

Arrange three squares of foil per onion. Place the onion in the centre of the layers of foil, bring the edges up and together over the top of the onion and twist lightly together.

Place around the edges of your charcoal fire or over the direct heat of a gas grill. Cook for 30–40 minutes, until the onions are tender to the prick of a small sharp knife.

Remove from the fire and carefully untwist the foil. Gently prise open the onions and divide the remaining butter and vinegar among them. Taste with your fingers and correct the seasoning.

Rewrap the onions and allow them to cook for a further 10 minutes.

Once cooked, remove the onions from the heat and allow them to stand for a few minutes. Remove from the foil and transfer to a serving plate.

To serve, gently squeeze the bottom of the onions as you would a baked potato, so they open a little.

BROCCOLI
AND
SPINACH
'COUSCOUS'

This super-healthy salad is fantastic for all barbecue occasions.

Wash and drain the broccoli. Finely slice the florets from the stalk (discarding the stalk), to create a couscous-like texture with the broccoli flowers.

Place the spinach leaves on a large platter, or into a salad dish.

Arrange the avocado slices on top, then the broccoli and pine nuts.

Scatter with the basil and parmesan. Season lightly with salt flakes and pepper.

At the last minute, dress and toss with the lime juice. Serve straight away.

SERVES 4–6

½ head broccoli

250 g baby spinach leaves, washed

2 avocados, peeled and sliced

½ cup toasted pine nuts

1 cup picked sweet basil

100 g parmesan, sliced using a vegetable peeler

salt flakes

freshly ground black pepper

juice of 2 limes

SPICED
POTATO
AND
CHICKPEA
DOSA

MAKES 4

DOSA BATTER

1 cup besan (chickpea flour)

1 cup plain flour

pinch of salt

1 teaspoon bicarbonate of soda

½ teaspoon yellow mustard seeds

½ teaspoon black mustard seeds

FILLING

1 tablespoon sunflower oil

1 onion, diced

salt

1 teaspoon ginger paste

1 teaspoon garlic paste

½ teaspoon ground cumin

½ teaspoon ground coriander

½ teaspoon ground turmeric

2 potatoes, peeled, diced
and boiled until tender

100 g tinned chickpeas, drained

2 ripe tomatoes, roughly chopped

½ cup frozen peas, thawed

freshly ground black pepper

½ cup chopped mint

½ cup chopped coriander leaves

This a great vego feast, straight off the barbecue. And because it's cooked on a Teflon sheet on the barbecue, there's no cross-contamination with any meat — so the carnivores are safe! You can buy non-stick Teflon sheets at barbecue supply stores.

Combine all the batter ingredients in a bowl. Mix in about 375 ml (1½ cups) water and whisk thoroughly. Leave to rest while you prepare the filling.

Heat the oil in a pan. Sauté the onion with a pinch of salt until soft. Add the ginger, garlic and ground spices and sauté until aromatic.

Add the potatoes and chickpeas and combine well to thoroughly mix the flavours.

Add the tomatoes and peas and mix again. Remove from the heat and season with salt and pepper. Finally, add the fresh herbs.

To make the dosas, heat the plate of your barbecue to medium heat. Place a non-stick Teflon sheet on the plate. Using a ladle, pour about one-quarter of the batter onto the Teflon sheet or judge the amount by how big your non-stick sheet is, as they can vary in size. In any case, you will need to cook the dosa in batches.

Quickly work the batter into a rough circle, using a spatula. When the mixture begins to bubble and the top is almost dry, place one-quarter of the filling in the centre. Using tongs, lift the Teflon sheet and roll the dosa over on itself, to make a roll.

Repeat with the remaining batter and filling. Arrange the cooked dosa on a platter, keeping it warm as you cook the rest. These dosa go well with the Barbecued pepper chicken curry (page 172) and Spiced red bean salad (page 88).

MARINATED
OLIVES

These olives are a great little addition to a barbecue. They can be served as tasty finger food while the meat, fish and veg are cooking, or as a side dish to accompany the main show. They are also delicious on Bruschetta (page 18).

For the best result use a mixture of olives — black and green, large and small — and try to buy them unpitted. If you have any marinated olives left over, they can be pureed with extra virgin olive oil and made into a tapenade.

Combine the olives with the remaining ingredients and leave to stand for 1 hour.

The olives will keep for up to 1 week in the refrigerator if stored in an airtight container, but are best eaten within a few days.

MAKES 500 G

100 g manzanillo olives, washed and pitted

100 g kalamata olives, washed and pitted

100 g ligurian or niçoise olives, washed and pitted

100 g queen green olives, washed and pitted

zest and juice of 1 lemon

1 fennel bulb, washed and finely sliced

½ cup chopped celery heart (including leaves and stalk)

small handful roughly chopped mint

1 garlic clove, finely sliced

80 ml (⅓ cup) olive oil

1 teaspoon toasted cumin seeds

1 teaspoon chopped red chilli

BARBECUED AVOCADO
WITH
HERB LABNEH SALAD

SERVES 4–6

4 firm but ripe avocados

200 g labneh

juice of 1 lemon

2 tablespoons extra virgin olive oil

¼ cup dill

¼ cup basil

¼ cup coriander leaves and a little soft stem from the top leaves

¼ cup mint

salt flakes

freshly cracked black pepper

This recipe works well with slightly firm avocados, but the real key is having a super-hot and clean barbecue.

Labneh is a cheese made from yoghurt. It is nice and sharp, which goes really well with the creaminess of the avocado.

Prepare your barbecue for direct cooking over a high heat. Make sure it's free of any dirt — you don't want to be chewing grit!

Cut all your avocados in half and remove the stones. Leaving the skin on, cut the halves into halves again if using smaller avocados, or into thirds if using larger ones. Set aside.

Place the labneh in a bowl. Add half the lemon juice and half the olive oil and beat to loosen the cheese. The mixture does not need to be completely combined.

Roughly chop the herbs and mix half into the cheese. Reserve the rest to sprinkle over at the end.

Barbecue the avocado pieces with the skin still on, laying them cut side down so they are flush with the grill surface. Once charred, turn them over gently and cook the other side.

Remove from the barbecue to a serving board or platter. Remove the skin from the charred avocado.

Dollop the labneh mixture all over the avocado, then sprinkle with the remaining herbs. Combine the remaining olive oil and lemon juice and dress the salad liberally.

Season with salt flakes and pepper. This is best served straight away.

PANZANELLA

This traditional Tuscan salad is served in summer when tomatoes are at their ripest and basil is at its most aromatic. These top-quality ingredients are bound with fantastic extra virgin olive oil, for, like most great salads, panzanella is only equal to the sum of its parts.

I love panzanella, as it goes so well with everything: you can serve it with seafood such as prawns, lobster and squid; with meat, either chicken or lamb; or as a stand-alone salad. I like to use overripe tomatoes, as they are juiciest. If you like, to finish you could add some Marinated fire-roasted peppers (page 52), half a dozen anchovies and some fresh buffalo mozzarella.

Pull the prepared bruschetta into chunks or large pieces and place in a bowl.

Halve the tomatoes and squeeze the seeds and juice through a sieve into a separate bowl. Discard the seeds and keep the juice for the dressing. Break up the tomatoes.

Rip half the basil into a mortar, along with the garlic and a good pinch of salt. Pound to a pulp. Add the red wine vinegar and reserved tomato juice. Gradually add the olive oil and adjust the seasoning.

Combine the broken bread with the broken tomatoes, then add the basil dressing and squeeze together to combine all the flavours.

To finish, add the rocket and remaining basil leaves, and toss together. Serve straight away.

SERVES 6

½ quantity Bruschetta (page 18)

500 g overripe vine-ripened tomatoes

1 small bunch basil, leaves picked

2 garlic cloves, peeled

salt

2 tablespoons red wine vinegar

100 ml best-quality extra virgin olive oil

freshly ground black pepper

handful wide-leaf rocket

COLESLAW

125 ml (½ cup) cider vinegar

½ cup sugar

800 g white, savoy or red cabbage

3 large celery stalks

1 tablespoon dijon mustard

½ teaspoon celery seeds

2 firm red apples, finely sliced into matchsticks

3–4 tablespoons Greek yoghurt

½ cup roughly chopped mint

salt

freshly ground black pepper

Coleslaw is one of those dishes that has had so many variations over time that the true original has been lost — and I'm certainly not saying that this is it!

Needless to say, coleslaw has become part of barbecue folklore, as it goes so well with barbecued meat and fish. Originally, before the invention of mayonnaise, it was made with a vinegar-based dressing. This recipe gives a healthy twist to the mayo-based varieties around these days. If you prefer mayo, then knock yourself out and use it!

I prefer to use firm white cabbage, but you can substitute savoy or use red cabbage for colour.

Place the vinegar and sugar in a small saucepan and bring to the boil to dissolve the sugar. Remove from the heat and allow to cool.

While the vinegar mix is cooling, finely slice the cabbage and celery using a sharp knife or a Japanese mandoline.

When the vinegar mixture has cooled, add the dijon mustard and celery seeds, then combine with the cabbage and celery. For the best result, leave this to stand overnight in order to extract the most flavour. Otherwise, allow it to stand for at least 2–3 hours.

Before serving, add the apple, yoghurt and mint, and season to taste.

CARROT
SALAD

When I was travelling through Morocco, I loved seeing the donkeys pulling little carts full of carrots, coriander and parsley, hustling their way through the open markets and souks. Carrot salad is very common in Morocco, and the subtlety of its flavour marries well with North African–style brazier-cooked lamb kofte and skewers.

This is a great salad and it is so easy to make. The secret is in the cooking of the carrots; they have to be done whole, as this way they retain more of their sweetness and taste. Also, try to choose carrots that are organic and fresh, with a good snap. Crushing the garlic with salt keeps the flavours subtle.

Boil the carrots in salty water until tender. Drain, and allow to cool a little so you can slice them into similar-sized pieces.

Place the garlic cloves in a mortar and crush with a little salt.

Add the toasted cumin seeds and continue to pound just a little to combine the flavours.

Add the honey and lemon juice. Combine, then toss the carrots thoroughly in the garlic mixture. Add the raisins, pine nuts and coriander.

Dress with a little olive oil, season with pepper and allow to stand at room temperature for 1 hour or so to let the flavours settle together.

Serve the salad at room temperature.

SERVES 6

1 kg carrots, peeled

salt

3 garlic cloves, peeled

1½ teaspoons toasted cumin seeds

1 teaspoon honey

juice of 1 lemon

2 teaspoons raisins

2 teaspoons pine nuts, lightly toasted

1 bunch coriander, washed and chopped

olive oil

freshly ground black pepper

PINEAPPLE, CUCUMBER AND CHILLI SALAD

½ sweet ripe pineapple
(I recommend the jagged-leaf variety)

2 telegraph (long) cucumbers

1 tablespoon lime-infused macadamia oil
(optional)

½ cup roughly chopped mint

freshly ground black pepper

1–2 red chillies, seeded and thinly sliced

This salad is pretty versatile. With its freshness and sweetness, it works with Mexican and South-East Asian dishes — well, just about everything on the barbecue.

Peel the pineapple and remove the core and spiky eyes. Cut the flesh into small cubes.

Peel and seed the cucumber, then dice the same size as the pineapple.

Toss together and dress with the macadamia oil, if using. Place in a serving bowl.

Add the mint and season with pepper.

Garnish with sliced chilli.

This salad is best when fresh as the ingredients maintain their crispness — but it is still delicious the next day.

VIETNAMESE
RICE NOODLE
SALAD

I have included this dish because it's one of my wife's favourites. Travelling through Vietnam she fell in love with the food and its fresh flavours. I love this dish because it's quick and simple and tastes just awesome.

This salad is wonderfully refreshing on its own, but to make it more substantial you can also add any meat that has been marinated, grilled and finely sliced.

Prepare the noodles by adding them to a saucepan of boiling water and cooking for 2–3 minutes. Drain, refresh with cold water and drain again.

Place the lettuce on a large platter, or divide among bowls, depending on how you wish to serve. Pile the noodles on top.

Arrange the cucumber and carrot around the side, and the bean sprouts in the middle.

Scatter with the herbs and peanuts.

Dress liberally with the Nuoc cham sauce and sprinkle with chillies.

This is best eaten straight away.

SERVES 4–6

250 g vermicelli rice noodles

¼ iceberg lettuce, finely sliced

1 cucumber, peeled, seeded and cut into sticks or slices

1 carrot, cut into thin matchsticks

200 g bean sprouts

½ bunch coriander, leaves chopped

½ bunch mint, leaves chopped

100 g roasted unsalted peanuts

1 quantity Nuoc cham sauce (page 271)

chopped red chillies

STUFFED
GEM
SQUASH

SERVES 6

6 fist-sized gem squash, washed

½ quantity Marinated olives (page 69)

6 semi-dried tomatoes

100 g feta, cubed

I first encountered gem squash when I was travelling and surfing my way around South Africa. I pretty much had them with every meal. They were sometimes referred to as cricket ball squash, as they resemble a cricket ball in size. Whenever there was a braai (barbecue) happening at whatever backpackers I was staying at, the squash would be stabbed with a knife and put on coals to roast. When they were cooked, the top would be cut off, the seeds scooped out and a knob of butter placed inside, along with a little salt and pepper.

Later, when I was at the River Café, we served them as antipasti, stuffed with olives and sun-dried tomatoes, which certainly added a different dimension. As an alternative you could use spaghetti squash, small onion squash or pumpkins.

Prepare your barbecue for cooking over a medium heat.

Prick each squash with a metal skewer, inserted from the top into the centre. Place the squash around the coals, or directly over the heat of a gas barbecue, and cook until tender.

When cooked and cooled a little, use a serrated knife to cut the top off each squash, cutting about a quarter of the way down. Scoop out the seeds, and reserve the tops to use as lids.

Combine the marinated olives with the tomatoes and feta, and divide between the squash, filling right to the top. Place the lids on top and serve.

KIMCHI

Kimchi is the cornerstone of a Korean barbecue. Traditionally, it's served as a side dish and in dishes such as kimchi jjigae (kimchi soup). Kimchi is fermented pickled vegetables (commonly Chinese cabbage, radish, garlic and spring onions), plus chilli, ginger and salt. It has great health properties and is wonderful for digestion. Other cultures have something similar; for example, sauerkraut from Germany.

If you're going to attempt a Korean barbecue you have to have kimchi. You can buy it from Asian grocery stores, but why not try making it yourself? The great thing about this recipe is that the kimchi lasts for ages, and is at its best after six months. It's a long time to wait, but it gives you time to plan your Korean barbecue!

Wash the chopped cabbage. Drain, then sprinkle with the salt and allow to stand for a minimum of 2 hours.

Rinse the cabbage and squeeze out all the excess liquid. Place the cabbage in a large bowl and add the spring onions, garlic, chilli powder, ginger and sugar. Toss so the cabbage pieces are well coated with the other ingredients, then pack into a large sterilised glass jar.

Rinse the bowl that held the cabbage with hot water and swish it around to pick up all the flavours. Pour into the jar and seal with a tightly fitting lid. Place in a cool room for 2–3 days to start the fermentation process, then refrigerate or leave in a cool dark cupboard for a minimum of 2 months. For best results, leave for 6 months.

MAKES 500 G

1 large Chinese cabbage, chopped into 5 cm slices

100 g good-quality sea salt

8 spring onions, finely chopped

4 garlic cloves, peeled

2 tablespoons hot chilli powder

1 heaped teaspoon grated fresh ginger

1 tablespoon sugar

SUGAR LOAF CABBAGE
CORIANDER
AND
MINT SALAD

SERVES 4–6

½ sugar loaf cabbage, finely shredded

1 red onion, finely sliced

1 cup coriander leaves

1 cup mint

salt

freshly ground black pepper

lime juice, to taste

I love the crunch contrast of this salad. The sweetness of the sugar loaf cabbage (that's the pointy variety) and the zesty freshness of lime juice and herbs make it the perfect partner for barbecued fish and white meat. If you can't get hold of a sugar loaf cabbage, a savoy cabbage will do the job.

Combine all the vegetables and herbs together. Season with salt and pepper.

Dress at the last moment with lime juice and serve straight away.

CRUNCHY CUCUMBER
MINT
AND
CHILLI SALAD

This very refreshing salad goes well with many styles of grilled meat and fish. If serving it with non-Asian meals, just dress the salad with lime juice.

For best results, use a speed peeler to peel your cucumbers on all four sides, stopping when you reach the seeds. (If you don't have a speed peeler, a standard vegetable peeler will also work.)

Place the thin strips of cucumber into a bowl filled with ice water. Allow to stand for 10 minutes to thoroughly chill and crisp up.

When ready to serve, drain the cucumbers well and place on a serving platter.

Scatter with the mint and the rinsed chilli.

Dress lightly with Nam prik pla and serve straight away.

SERVES 4–6

2 telegraph (long) cucumbers

1 cup mint

1 red chilli, finely sliced, rinsed
in cold water and drained

Nam prik pla (page 270), for dressing

SOM TAM:
GREEN PAPAYA
SALAD

SERVES 4

2 dark green papaya, peeled and grated

1 cup green beans, chopped into 2 cm lengths

6 green bird's eye chillies

3 garlic cloves, peeled

25 g dried shrimp, rinsed in hot water and drained

50 g unsalted roasted peanuts

60 ml (¼ cup) lime juice

25 ml fish sauce

10 ml tamarind juice

2 ripe tomatoes, quartered

I love the flavours of Thai food — the insatiable heat, and the distinctive combination of sweet, salty and sour. It's like a sensory running of the bulls! Those machismo-destroying little bird's eye and prik kii nuu (mouse-dropping) chillies can reduce the toughest person to tears, but the exhilaration gets your endorphins rising.

I think the use of unripe fruit is so interesting, and often wonder what prompted people to use fruit in this way. The crunchy freshness of the green papaya adds such a great textural dimension to this salad. And believe me, with six chillies in this recipe, you'll need it! Use fewer chillies if you prefer less heat.

Som tam is often served with one of my favourite barbecued chicken dishes, Gai yang (page 214), along with sticky rice. The salad has quite a liquid consistency, but the juices are lovely soaked up by the rice and chicken.

Rinse the grated papaya in cold water and drain. Combine with the beans.

Combine the chillies and garlic in a mortar, and pound to a paste.

Separately, pound the shrimp with the peanuts. You want a crumbly texture, not a paste.

Combine the lime juice, fish sauce and tamarind juice with the chilli and garlic. Check the seasoning: you may need to add more fish sauce or lime juice, as the salty and sour flavours need to be evenly balanced.

Add the papaya and beans to the dressing, along with the tomatoes. Gently pound to just soften the papaya.

To serve, top with the pounded shrimp and peanut.

SHAVED FENNEL AND CELERY SALAD

I can't remember exactly when I fell in love with fennel, but I know it was since I left Australia to go travelling. It was probably when I first experienced a Florentine finnochio — those plump, round, firm, crisp and bulbous fennels from Italy.

I love the fresh aniseed flavour of fennel, and it is an excellent digestive. I find that a fennel salad is the perfect antidote to rich barbecued meats. You can slice or shave fennel, or cut it into largish wedges to munch on.

This recipe is so simple and fresh, you'll keep making it whether you're having a barbecue or not. It also uses the pale inside leaves of celery.

Wash the fennel in cold water and remove any brown outer fronds. Pick the herb tops from the fennel and reserve for the salad.

Cut the fennel in half lengthwise and finely slice, cutting across the rings of the bulb. Finely chop the fennel tops and the celery then toss together.

Combine the yoghurt with the lemon juice and olive oil and season with salt.

Dress the fennel and celery with the yoghurt dressing and serve.

SERVES 4

2 large firm round fennel bulbs

1 cup pale celery leaves and stems, washed

2 tablespoons biodynamic yoghurt

1 tablespoon lemon juice

1 tablespoon extra virgin olive oil

pinch of salt

TABOULEH

You can't have Lebanese food without tabouleh. It's the heart and soul of the meal. Serve the fresh flavours of flat-leaf parsley, lemon, burghul (bulgur wheat) and chopped tomato with lovely flat breads, hummus and grilled marinated meats. Talk about healthy and delicious.

SERVES 4

1 cup soaked fine burghul (bulgur wheat)

3 garlic cloves, chopped

1 large bunch flat-leaf parsley,
washed and roughly chopped

250 g tomatoes, halved, seeded and chopped

juice of 1 large lemon

salt

freshly ground black pepper

Wash and prepare the burghul as recommended on the packet. (Generally, place the burghul in a bowl, cover with cold water and set aside for 1 hour to soak.)

Mix the garlic and parsley in a bowl, then add the chopped tomatoes.

Drain and add the burghul and the lemon juice, and combine. Season with salt and pepper.

SPICED RED BEAN SALAD

I do yoga with a Geordie mate of mine called John, who spent a bit of time travelling through India. He cooked a wonderful dinner for me and my wife, and this recipe was part of the meal. I loved the pure, simple flavours and how they complemented the heat of the meat dishes.

This salad would go brilliantly with any of the spicy dishes in this book, particularly the Barbecued pepper chicken curry (page 172), Jerked chicken (page 164) and the sweet, smoky flavour of Classic barbecued sticky ribs (page 152) and Pamplona chicken (page 179).

SERVES 4

400 g can kidney beans, rinsed and drained

1 red onion, finely sliced

2 teaspoons toasted cumin seeds

1 bunch coriander, leaves and stems
washed and chopped

salt

freshly ground black pepper

juice of 1 lemon

Place the kidney beans and onion in a large bowl.

Add the toasted cumin seeds, then toss the chopped coriander through the salad.

Season with salt, pepper and lemon juice.

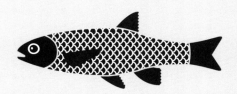

FISH
and
SEAFOOD

BEN'S CHILDHOOD FISH

WHOLE FISH THAI STYLE

SICILIAN SARDINES IN OIL

PAELLA

GRILLED LOBSTERS

MISO-BLACKENED FISH FILLETS

SALT-CRUSTED FISH IN COALS

INDIAN SPICE-CRUSTED FISH

MORETON BAY BUGS WITH FIGS AND
PANCETTA KEBABS

SCALLOPS WITH SWEET CHILLI JAM

DRUNKEN CRABS

**SNOWY MORRISON'S
HOT SMOKED SALMON**

CARIBBEAN JERKED RED FISH

**BARBECUED SPICE-CRUSTED TUNA
WITH TAHINI DRESSING**

BARBECUED TAMARIND PRAWNS

SURF CLAMS WITH BLACK PEPPER SAUCE

OYSTERS KILPATRICK MY WAY

LIME AND LEMONGRASS KING PRAWNS

BARBECUED CHILLI STINGRAY WINGS

CAPE TOWN KINGFISH FILLETS

KIWI BARBECUED TROUT WITH FIGS

SINGAPORE CHILLI CRABS

SQUID STUFFED WITH FENNEL AND BLACK
PUDDING

**BARBECUED CRISPY-SKIN
KING SALMON**

BARBECUED OYSTERS WITH XO SAUCE,
GINGER AND SHALLOT

BEN'S
CHILDHOOD
FISH

**FEEDS
2 HUNGRY
10-YEAR-OLDS**

1 whole fish
(perhaps a 700 g large bream),
gutted, scales left on

seaweed

This is not so much a recipe as a memory.

Build a fire and allow it to burn down to coals.

Stuff the fish with fresh seaweed — don't use old seaweed that's been washed up on the beach for a week!

Make a bed of even-sized, largish coals so the fish is kept out of the ash and dirt. Place the fish on top of the coals and cook for 6–8 minutes.

Using a stick, turn the fish over and cook for another 5–6 minutes.

The hard part is getting the fish off the coals and onto a flat stone. Use the seaweed to cover the stone like a plate. Pick off the blackened skin and get stuck in.

WHOLE FISH THAI STYLE

The inspiration for this dish comes from my wife and from David Thompson. I have known David since I was a young chef working in Sydney, and my wife worked for David as a junior restaurant manager at Nahm in London, and has travelled extensively through Thailand. Between them, they have prompted my obsession with Thai food.

This dish works best with a nice white-fleshed reef fish — a pan-sized snapper, coral trout or even a tasty bream. It's best to use a fish basket and cook over the direct heat of coals or gas.

The best and simplest way to serve the fish would be with plain steamed rice and Green papaya salad (page 86) to balance the sweet flavours.

Using a sharp knife, cut incisions along both sides of the fish, about 1 cm apart.

To make the marinade, place all the ingredients in a food processor and blend until smooth. Rub the fish with the marinade and place in the refrigerator for 30 minutes while you prepare your barbecue for direct cooking over a medium–high heat.

Lightly oil the fish basket. Place the fish inside then close and secure the basket. Place over direct heat and cook for 8 minutes on one side, then turn the fish basket over and cook for another 8 minutes.

Meanwhile, warm the chilli jam with a little water to make a brushable paste. When the fish has cooked, brush the fish liberally with the chilli jam paste and cook for a further 1–2 minutes on each side.

Remove the fish from the basket. Brush with any remaining jam and serve garnished with the lime leaves, coriander and lime wedges.

SERVES 4

1 whole fish (up to 2 kg),
such as snapper, scaled and cleaned
(ask your fishmonger to do this)

sunflower oil

5 tablespoons Thai sweet chilli jam
(page 270)

2 kaffir lime leaves, very finely sliced

2 tablespoons chopped coriander leaves

1 lime, cut into wedges

MARINADE

5 coriander roots, washed and chopped

8 garlic cloves, peeled

5 red Asian shallots, peeled

1 bird's eye chilli

1 tablespoon ground turmeric,
or finely chopped fresh turmeric

2 tablespoons ground white pepper

3–4 tablespoons fish sauce, to taste

2–3 tablespoons lime juice, to taste

60 ml (¼ cup) coconut cream
(skim the top off a cold can of coconut milk)

SICILIAN
SARDINES
IN OIL

SERVES 6

12 whole sardines, cleaned

salt

freshly ground black pepper

1 tablespoon crumbled wild oregano

1 dried chilli, crumbled

1 garlic clove, finely sliced

juice of 1 lemon, or to taste

250 ml (1 cup) best-quality extra virgin olive oil

Being a Western Australian, I love our famous sardines. It's no surprise that the Sicilians who migrated to WA felt right at home, and I am sure they kept the sardines their secret for some time.

I picked up this recipe from a fisherman in Fremantle by the name of Jim. It's a classic Italian recipe, using a technique called sott'olio, which means 'under oil'. The fish is simply grilled, seasoned and covered in good-quality olive oil.

These sardines are great served with Bruschetta (page 18) and some shaved fennel.

Prepare your barbecue for direct grilling.

Season the sardines and place them directly over the fire. Cook on each side for 3 minutes, then transfer to a shallow dish.

Scatter over the oregano, chilli and garlic.

Season with salt, pepper and a squeeze of lemon juice, and cover with olive oil.

Allow to cool and let the flavours mingle before serving.

PAELLA

Paella is Spain's national dish, and there are as many variations as there are for Italy's risotto. Paella is a celebration of ingredients from the land and the sea, but common to all varieties is saffron, with its beautiful aroma and striking colour.

The reason I have included this recipe here is because the best paellas are cooked in huge pans over the glowing embers of a fire. Excellent results can also be achieved with a good gas or kettle barbecue.

Steep the saffron in the wine for at least 10 minutes.

Heat the olive oil in a large pan or paella dish and sauté the chicken and chorizo until nicely coloured.

Add the onion, celery, dried chilli and garlic, and fry for 2 minutes.

Add the octopus, then sprinkle the rice over.

Pour the saffron-infused wine over the rice and allow to evaporate. Add the stock and shake the pan to disperse the ingredients.

Add the broad beans, prawns and mussels, and simmer for 15 minutes, shaking the pan every so often but not stirring. If the rice is just tender and the liquid has been absorbed, the paella is ready. If it is a little wet and the rice is still al dente, cook for a further 5 minutes.

Just before you remove the paella from the heat, add the tomatoes and stir them into the rice, turning everything over to plump it up.

To serve, season to taste and garnish with the parsley and lemon halves.

SERVES 4

good pinch of saffron

175 ml white wine

2 tablespoons olive oil

2 chicken thighs, boned and diced

150 g chorizo picante, sliced

1 onion, finely diced

100 g celery, finely diced

1 dried chilli, finely chopped

4 garlic cloves, sliced

12 baby octopus, cleaned and washed

250 g paella rice

1 litre (4 cups) chicken stock

150 g broad beans, podded

250 g raw prawns, unpeeled

12 black mussels

12 vine-ripened cherry tomatoes, lightly roasted

salt

freshly ground black pepper

2 tablespoons chopped flat-leaf or curly parsley

2 lemons, halved

GRILLED
LOBSTERS

SERVES 2

2 × 800–900 g live lobsters or crayfish

salt

freshly ground black pepper

4 bay leaves

½ quantity Herb butter (page 274)

This recipe was inspired by a New Year's Eve I once spent in Norfolk. In the UK they have fantastic native lobsters with big nippers and wonderfully sweet, tender flesh. We bought four largish lobsters but had little means of cooking them (i.e. pots!). I just added some wet bay leaves, wrapped the lobsters in foil and threw them into the log fire. Awesome.

This recipe has evolved slightly from the original, but it's the simplicity that defines this dish. Its success relies wholly on the availability of top-quality live lobsters. The only thing added is a fresh-flavoured Herb butter (page 274).

Kill your lobsters or crayfish by placing them in the freezer for 30 minutes to put them to sleep. Cut in half along the top from head to tail, and open into two halves. Remove the gravel sac (the blackish tube along the tail).

Season the halves with salt and pepper and push a bay leaf under the flesh of the tail.

Prepare your barbecue for direct grilling over a high heat.

Place the lobster halves, flesh side down, over the heat and cook for 4–5 minutes. Turn them over onto the shell side and continue to cook for 2–3 minutes. The flesh should be nicely charred.

To serve, remove the bay leaves and spoon some of the herb and garlic butter on top of each lobster half. Allow the butter to melt and serve straight away.

MISO-BLACKENED
FISH FILLETS

SERVES 6

1 quantity Miso marinade (page 268)

4 large fillets of flaky fish
(shark, mulloway or even snapper)

coriander and oregano leaves

This recipe features a classic Japanese miso marinade. Actually, it's more like a cure, as the salt and sugar work together to draw the moisture out of the fish. This helps to improve the texture of flaky fish and imparts a wonderful flavour.

Miso marinade was made famous in the West by the restaurant chain Nobu in its legendary black cod recipe. It also works well with chicken and pork, although you will need to leave it to marinate for longer. I use it with Robatayaki miso eggplant (page 44), and you can use it as a base to make dressings for salads and sashimi dishes.

Pour enough marinade over the fish fillets to cover them well. Cover and leave to marinate in the refrigerator for 8 hours or overnight, turning the fillets several times.

Remove the fillets from the marinade and allow to come to room temperature. Cut into large chunks or cubes and thread onto long metal skewers or pre-soaked bamboo skewers.

Prepare your barbecue for direct grilling over a medium–high heat.

Place the skewers above the coals, so the sugar in the miso marinade caramelises and blackens slightly. Cook for 6–8 minutes, turning the skewers regularly.

To serve, brush with a little unused marinade, and garnish with coriander and oregano.

SALT-CRUSTED
FISH
IN COALS

The hard part about cooking a fish whole is controlling the heat so the skin doesn't burn or stick to the grill. Cooking fish in a salt crust solves these problems, and keeps it deliciously moist. I like to serve this with Grilled verdure miste (page 43) and a nice Basil mayonnaise (page 273).

To prepare the salt crust, place the chopped lemons in a large bowl and add the salt, egg whites and fennel seeds. Mix well.

On a baking tray large enough to hold the fish, use half the salt mixture to make a bed 2–3 cm thick in the shape of the fish, and place the fish on top. Stuff the parsley into the cavity of the fish to prevent the salt getting in and making the flesh overly salty.

Preheat your gas barbecue to 180–200°C with the hood down or prepare a hot charcoal fire.

Cover the fish with the remaining salt, similar in thickness to the bottom layer of salt. If need be, use scrunched-up foil to make a retaining wall to hold the salt in place.

Place the fish on the barbecue and bake for 40–50 minutes with the lid down. If using coals, make a thin base of charcoal by moving the majority of the coals to the side of the fire. Place the tray onto this base, then pile the coals around the edge and on top of the fish.

Check that the fish is cooked by inserting a small knife or roasting fork into the thickest part of the fish; touch the knife or fork to your lips and if it's warm, the fish is done. Remove from the heat and allow to rest for 10 minutes before removing the crust.

Use a serrated knife to saw around the salt base, being careful not to cut into the flesh. Lift the top off; it may come away in one piece or break into several pieces. Brush any excess salt off the fish with a wet pastry brush.

To serve, peel back the skin and cut down the centre of the fish, removing the flesh in portions. It should be wonderfully moist.

SERVES 10

2 lemons, roughly chopped into 3 cm pieces

5 kg rock salt

2 egg whites, lightly whisked

2 tablespoons fennel seeds

1 × 2 kg whole fish (trout, salmon or barramundi), freshly gutted, gills removed

1 bunch flat-leaf parsley

INDIAN
SPICE-CRUSTED
FISH

This spice crust is fantastic. It's a sidestep away from your usual breadcrumb and nut combination, using dal (dried white and yellow split peas). On occasion I have used crushed chickpeas, and then it becomes more like a falafel crust. You can use the mixture with chicken breasts, but I think it's the perfect complement to a white fish fillet like bar cod. I just loved the texture and flavours of the dal. It's best to use home-dried curry leaves rather than bought ones for this dish, mainly for colour.

Serve with spiced yoghurt (page 160) and Spiced red bean salad (page 88), or with a nice sweet tomato relish to balance the spiciness of the fish.

Place all the marinade ingredients in a food processor and puree. Rub the fish fillets with the marinade.

Toast the crust ingredients, except the curry leaves and coriander, in a frying pan until the split peas turn golden and the spices release their aromas. Leave to cool, then pound in a mortar until you have a fine crumb. Crumble in the curry leaves and chopped coriander.

Roll the fish in the crust mixture.

Prepare your barbecue for direct grilling over a medium–high heat.

Add vegetable oil and cook the fish for 4–5 minutes on one side, then turn and cook for 3–4 minutes on the other.

Serve with lime wedges.

SERVES 4

4 thick white fish fillets, such as bar cod

vegetable oil

lime wedges

MARINADE

2 pinches salt

2 teaspoons chilli powder

juice of 1 lime

1 teaspoon sugar

2 teaspoons garlic paste

2 teaspoons ginger paste

CRUST

180 g white split peas (urad dal)

1 tablespoon yellow split peas (chana dal)

1 teaspoon fennel seeds

½ teaspoon cumin

1 teaspoon black peppercorns

½ teaspoon chilli flakes

20 freshly dried curry leaves

2 tablespoons chopped coriander leaves

MORETON BAY BUGS WITH FIGS AND PANCETTA KEBABS

SERVES 4

8 moreton bay bugs or slipper lobsters

200 g thinly sliced dried pancetta

8 bay leaves

4 ripe figs, halved

2 tablespoons olive oil

juice of 1 lemon, or to taste

I love bugs. They are truly one of the strangest-looking crustaceans we eat, but one of the tastiest — in my opinion, second only to wild marron. I cooked this dish on a TV cook-off series called *The Best in Australia*. Personally, I think it should have won! Everything about it works.

This combination of fruit, seafood and meat is quite common in the Mediterranean. Just make sure you have lovely ripe figs and fresh bugs. Ideally, the skewers should be cooked over a charcoal fire, but a regular grill will do.

Prepare your barbecue for direct grilling over a high heat.

Prepare the bugs or slipper lobsters by removing the meat from the shells. To do this, remove the head, use a pair of scissors to cut along each side under the tail, then pull out the flesh.

Take four metal skewers and thread the following onto each skewer: a bug's tail, some thinly sliced pancetta, a bay leaf and half a fig, then repeat the sequence to complete the skewer.

Brush the skewers with a little oil and place over a high heat to cook until the bugs are translucent, the thin pancetta is crisp and the figs are oozy and caramelised.

To serve, dress with a squeeze of lemon juice.

SCALLOPS
with
SWEET CHILLI JAM

Scallops are one of my favourite shellfish to grill. They have a magical effect at a barbecue — people just can't get enough of them. Here, their sweet, salty flavour is a perfect match with chilli jam, balanced by the freshness of the salad garnish. They are a great little starter or taster to pass around for a sophisticated evening around the flames. Remember to keep the shells for serving.

Prepare your barbecue hotplate for grilling over a medium–high heat.

Season the scallops just prior to cooking.

Lightly oil the barbecue hotplate and place the scallops on it, flat side down. Cook for 1 minute, then turn them over.

Spoon on the chilli jam and toss the scallops through it so they are well coated. Remove from the heat after no more than 3 minutes on the grill, less if the scallops are small. High heat is the key to cooking scallops quickly.

Return the jam-coated scallops to their shells. Toss together the mint, lime leaves, lemongrass and green chilli, if using.

To serve, garnish each shell with a little of the mint salad and a lime wedge.

SERVES 4

12 large king scallops, cleaned and shelled

salt

freshly ground black pepper

sunflower oil

4–5 tablespoons Thai sweet chilli jam (page 270)

1 cup mint

3 kaffir lime leaves, finely sliced

1 lemongrass stem, white part only, finely sliced

1 green chilli (optional), finely sliced

12 lime wedges

DRUNKEN CRABS

SERVES 4

4 large blue swimmer crabs or sand crabs, cleaned and halved, claws cracked

375 ml can beer, or 100 ml vodka

3 garlic cloves, chopped

2 hot red chillies

2 cups chopped spring onions, the white and green parts chopped separately

2 tablespoons olive oil

400 g can chopped roma (plum) tomatoes, drained

1 cup chopped coriander leaves

salt

freshly ground black pepper

When I was a first-year apprentice I worked what we called the backbench, doing the prep for the section chef de parties. Along with a million other tasks, I would spend the services prepping live crabs, soaking them in beer or vodka and setting them up for the chef to cook. You had to stay ahead of the chef, otherwise you would get stuff thrown at you. It wasn't long before I was the section chef doing exactly the same thing, throwing things at the apprentice if he didn't keep ahead! You can cook this dish on a hotplate or in a wok balanced on coals, and it's great served with crusty bread spread with loads of butter.

Place the cleaned crabs in a bowl with the beer or vodka and leave them to steep for 10 minutes.

Preheat your barbecue hotplate to a high heat. Splash some beer onto the hotplate or wok to check the heat; the beer should evaporate quickly, but let it heat up for a further 5 minutes just to make sure.

Combine the garlic, chillies and white spring onions in a large bowl, together with the steeped crabs.

Pour the olive oil on the hotplate or wok, then add the crabs and pour over the chopped tomatoes. Place a bowl or the lid of the wok over the crabs, then pour the beer or vodka marinade around the edge of the bowl so the liquid seeps underneath and steams them. Allow to steam for 5 minutes. Remove the cover to check how they're going by breaking a section of crab. When the meat is white, toss through the remaining green tops of the spring onions and the coriander.

Check the seasoning and remove to a serving plate.

SNOWY MORRISON'S HOT SMOKED SALMON

SERVES 4

4 × 200 g thick salmon fillets,
bones removed, skin left on

1 tablespoon dark rum

SNOWY'S SECRET RUB

1 tablespoon soft brown sugar

1 tablespoon Cajun spice (page 276)

1 tablespoon salt flakes

1 tablespoon tomato ketchup

1 tablespoon low-salt soy sauce

I named my son after my mate Herb (aka Stephen) Barrett, who grew up on the west coast of Tasmania. We spent some time with Herb and his family when we were filming Surfing the Menu, and were introduced to a long-time family friend called Snowy Morrison.

Snowy is a legend. He runs the wood mill down in Strahan, and while we were filming with him he made some of the most amazing hot smoked salmon I have ever tasted. We asked Snowy in vain to give up his recipe. Finally, with the help of Herb, I uncovered the long-kept secrets of this old dog's smoked salmon.

For the real deal you'll need to get your hands on some Tasmanian cheesewood woodchips, but Snowy says you can use a fruit wood like cherry or apple. I've had great success with Jack Daniel's wood smoking chips made from the barrel. Whichever woodchips you use, they'll need to be pre-soaked. You'll also need a kettle barbecue, as that's what Snowy uses.

To make the rub, combine the sugar, Cajun spice and salt, then mix in the ketchup and soy sauce.

Wash the salmon with the rum and leave to marinate for 30 minutes. Massage in the secret rub and leave to marinate in the refrigerator for 2 hours.

Remove the salmon from the refrigerator and allow it to come to room temperature.

Prepare a kettle barbecue for indirect cooking, building a small coal fire on both sides of the grill and allowing it to burn quite low until almost out. Add two handfuls of pre-soaked woodchips to both sides and allow them to start smoking well, with the lid on. If you have a thermometer, the temperature should be around 80–100°C.

Place the salmon on the grill, away from the heat source. Replace the lid and smoke for 40 minutes. Do not lift the lid, because if you're looking, you're not cooking!

Check the fish after 40 minutes, when it should be just cooked. Remove from the barbecue and allow it to rest before serving.

CARIBBEAN
JERKED
RED FISH

The thing I loved about living in Hackney in London is its cultural diversity. There are Turkish mini-marts, kebab stalls, Chinese restaurants, Vietnamese grocery stores and Nigerian and Ghanaian takeaways. One of the great London foodie landmarks is the Ridley Road Market in Dalston. This recipe is a tribute to the wonderful flavours, sights and sounds of that effervescent market and the fabulous West Indian ingredients available. I especially love the reef fish you can buy there — red fish, rascasse and red snapper, all with lovely white flesh.

When barbecuing a whole fish it can be difficult to turn it over without pulling off half a fillet, as they tend to stick to the grill. I find it's much easier if you use a fish basket. It's basically a fish-shaped cage that holds your fish and enables you to turn it while the flames and the heat crisp up the skin, and it also allows you to baste your fish while cooking. It's a great thing to take along on fishing and camping trips.

Place all the jerk spice ingredients in a food processor and puree.

Make diagonal cuts into the skin of the fish. Rub in the marinade and leave for 30 minutes.

Prepare your barbecue for direct cooking over a medium–high heat.

Lightly oil the fish basket. Place the fish inside then close and secure the basket. Place over direct heat and cook for 10 minutes on one side, then turn the fish basket over and cook for another 10 minutes.

To test if the fish is cooked, push a skewer through the thickest part of the fish. It should pass through without much force.

Serve with lime wedges.

SERVES 4

1 whole red snapper or similar red reef fish (about 1.5 kg), scaled and gutted

sunflower oil

lime wedges

JERK SPICE

1½ cups chopped spring onions

1 cup chopped coriander leaves

2 Scotch bonnet chillies

60 ml (¼ cup) lime juice

1 tablespoon cider vinegar

1 tablespoon brown sugar

2 teaspoons thyme

1 teaspoon ginger paste

1½ teaspoons salt

1 teaspoon ground allspice or ground pimento

1 teaspoon freshly ground black pepper

½ teaspoon ground nutmeg

½ teaspoon ground cinnamon

BARBECUED
SPICE-CRUSTED
TUNA
WITH
TAHINI DRESSING

Many people have a bee in their bonnet about serving tuna — the catchcry 'sustainable fish' always come up. Well, just make sure your tuna is local line-caught fish!

Prepare your barbecue for direct grilling over a high heat.

To make the spice crust, roughly pound the coriander, cumin and sesame seeds in a mortar with the ras el hanout. Spread the spices on a chopping board or tray and season with salt and pepper.

In the same mortar, smash the garlic clove with a little salt, then add the tahini. Mix with the pestle, then add a little water to thin the mixture to the consistency of thick pouring cream. Add the olive oil and the juice of one lemon and season to taste with salt and pepper.

Rub the tuna steaks with the remaining lemon juice. Push the tuna into the spice mixture so the steaks are well coated on both sides.

Place the tuna steaks directly on the barbecue and cook on both sides until the tuna is medium-rare. The cooking time will depend on the thickness of the tuna – the best way is to watch the colour change from red to white on the edge of the fish while cooking. When the colour change reaches the middle of the fish edge, turn and repeat the process.

Remove the tuna from the grill. Break it up roughly and arrange on a platter with the salad. Drizzle with the tahini dressing and serve straight away.

SERVES 4

1 garlic clove, peeled

salt

2 tablespoons tahini

80 ml (⅓ cup) extra virgin olive oil

juice of 2 lemons

freshly ground black pepper

4 × 150 g tuna loin steaks
(also look for bincho or albacore tuna)

grilled vegetable salad, or Grilled verdure miste
(page 43), to serve

SPICE CRUST

4 tablespoons coriander seeds

1 teaspoon cumin seeds

1 teaspoon sesame seeds

1 teaspoon ras el hanout

salt

freshly ground black pepper

BARBECUED
TAMARIND
PRAWNS

SERVES 4

550 g fresh large tiger prawns

2 tablespoons tamarind paste

2 tablespoons kecap manis

1 tablespoon palm sugar

1 tablespoon freshly ground black pepper

lime wedges

1 small bunch coriander, trimmed (optional)

2–4 fresh green chillies, seeded and quartered lengthways (optional)

Prepare your barbecue – preferably a charcoal barbecue grill – for cooking over a high heat. (You can also cook these prawns on a flat barbecue plate.)

Rinse the prawns well, then pat dry with a clean cloth. Using a sharp knife, make an incision along the outside curve of the tail. Remove the vein.

In a bowl, mix together the tamarind paste, kecap manis, palm sugar and pepper.

Pour the mixture over the prawns, rubbing it over the shells and into the incision in the tails. Cover and marinate for 1 hour.

Remove the prawns from the marinade and place on a rack over the charcoal grill or barbecue.

Grill the prawns for about 3 minutes on each side, brushing them with marinade as they cook.

Serve straight away, with lime wedges, and coriander and chillies if desired.

SURF
CLAMS
WITH
BLACK PEPPER
SAUCE

Diamond shell clams are very similar to pippies, vongole or English cockles. The diamond shell surf clams I use come from NZ and are an internationally recognised sustainable fishery off the South Island in Cloudy Bay (where great wine also comes from). They are sweet and tender and well worth trying. Diamond shell clams are available in vacuum-pack bags from most good fish mongers. All you need to do is cut the bag open and off you go! No cleaning required.

Prepare your flat barbecue plate for direct cooking over a high heat.

Next, make the sauce, as the clams will only take seconds to cook.

Heat the oil in a saucepan. Firstly fry the curry leaves for 1–2 minutes, until fragrant, then add the ginger paste, garlic paste, chilli and the spring onion whites. Fry gently for a minute.

Combine the kecap manis, oyster sauce, soy sauce and stock, then add to the pan. Bring to the boil, then reduce the heat and simmer for a few minutes.

Combine the cornflour and water to make a smooth paste. Slowly whisk in enough of the cornflour paste into the sauce until it is thick and coats the back of a spoon — you may not need it all.

Finally, whisk in the butter. Add the pepper and keep warm until needed.

Place the clams directly onto the hot barbecue griddle plate and place a heatproof bowl over the top to steam them. Cook for just a minute or two, until the clams open up. Once cooked, scoop up the clams and place them in a bowl.

Pour the warm sauce all over the clams. Garnish with the spring onion greens and coriander. Serve straight away, with steamed rice.

SERVES 4

1 kg surf clams (I use diamond shell clams from New Zealand)

chopped greens of 3 spring onions

1 loose cup coriander leaves

steamed rice, to serve

BLACK PEPPER SAUCE

2 tablespoons sunflower oil

¼ cup fresh curry leaves

1 tablespoon ginger paste

1 tablespoon garlic paste

1 long red chilli, chopped

chopped whites of 3 spring onions

2 tablespoons kecap manis

2 tablespoons oyster sauce

2 tablespoons light soy sauce

250 ml (1 cup) chicken stock

2 tablespoons cornflour

80 ml (⅓ cup) water

50 g butter

2 tablespoons freshly cracked black pepper

OYSTERS
KILPATRICK
MY WAY

500 g smoked streaky bacon, diced

24 shucked oysters, on the shell
(Pacific oysters are best for cooking)

rock salt (optional)

lime wedges

SAUCE

125 ml (½ cup) ketchup

125 ml (½ cup) HP sauce

1 tablespoon creamed horseradish

1 teaspoon Hot chilli sauce (page 263),
or similar habanero chilli sauce

2 tablespoons lime juice

freshly ground black pepper

Prepare your barbecue for indirect cooking over a high heat.

Fry your bacon until crisp, reserving the drippings from the pan. Allow the bacon to cool.

Mix all the sauce ingredients in a small bowl. Taste and adjust the flavours as desired.

Spoon about 1 teaspoon of the sauce over each oyster, then top with the crisp bacon and reserved bacon drippings.

Place the oyster shells between the barbecue grill bars, resting them so they don't tip over. If you find this difficult, just scrunch up some foil on a baking tray to create a bed for the shells, then push the oysters onto it.

Close the hood on your barbecue and cook for about 5 minutes, until the oysters are done. If your barbecue doesn't have a hood, you can cover the oysters with a heatproof bowl or bowls.

Arrange the oysters on a platter over a bed of rock salt, or on a serving dish lined with scrunched-up foil.

Serve straight away, with lime wedges.

LIME AND LEMONGRASS KING PRAWNS

These prawns are a classy snack or canapé, and also make a great starter dish when served with the Pickled cucumber, mint and chilli salad (page 85). A friend of ours, Tara Collins, nailed this recipe, and I nicked it off her!

Ideally these prawns are best cooked over a hot charcoal barbecue, but a hot gas barbecue will also do the job.

Soak 24 bamboo skewers for 1 hour in some water.

Prepare your barbecue for direct grilling over a high heat, or prepare a hot charcoal fire.

Place the lemongrass, lime leaves, chilli, oil and a pinch of salt in a small blender. Pulse until finely chopped. Toss the prawns in the marinade, cover and set aside for 1 hour to marinate in the fridge.

Thread the prawns onto your soaked skewers, from the tail end first.

Place the prawns directly on the barbecue, or on a rack over the charcoal grill. Grill the prawns for about 3 minutes, turning so they cook evenly, brushing them with the coconut milk, using the lemongrass trimmings as a brush.

Serve straight away.

SERVES 4–6

2 lemongrass stems, white part only, chopped (reserve the trimmings to use as a brush)

4 kaffir lime leaves, roughly chopped

2 long red chillies, roughly chopped

2 tablespoons vegetable oil

salt

24 large king prawns, shelled and deveined, tails left on

80 ml (⅓ cup) coconut milk

BARBECUED
CHILLI
STINGRAY
WINGS

2 stingray or skate wings
(as fresh as possible)

1 lemon

salt

1 tablespoon sunflower oil,
plus extra for greasing

1 tablespoon tamarind paste

1 tablespoon sugar

1 large piece of banana leaf in two sections,
enough to wrap the wings (if not available,
use foil and baking paper)

½ red onion, finely sliced

½ bunch coriander

1 lime, quartered

SPICE PASTE

1 tablespoon shrimp paste
(belacan — the smelly stuff!)

2 tablespoons sambal oelek

6 red Asian shallots, roughly chopped

5 garlic cloves, peeled

3 cm piece fresh ginger, roughly chopped

2 lemongrass stems, white part only,
roughly chopped

3 dried long chillies,
reconstituted in hot water

If you've ever been to Singapore, you may have heard of, or even tasted, their iconic chilli stingray. It's probably one of the most famous barbecue dishes in Asia, so it's well worth having a crack at it at home — it's a little cheaper than flying to Singapore!

It's important that your stingray wings are very fresh.

Rub the stingray with lemon juice and a good pinch of salt. Set aside for 5–10 minutes.

Place all the spice paste ingredients in a blender and puree.

Heat the oil in a saucepan and fry the spice paste for about 3 minutes, until fragrant. Add the tamarind paste, sugar and salt to taste. Reduce the heat and simmer until the sauce has slightly thickened. Remove and leave to cool.

Soften the banana leaf pieces over a flame or by pouring boiling water over them. Wipe with a wet cloth to cool and clean. Lightly oil the leaf with sunflower oil.

Spread half the spice paste over the banana leaf pieces. Place each of the stingray wings on top of a banana leaf piece then spoon the remaining paste over the fish. Fold each of the leaf pieces into a parcel and secure with toothpicks.

Preheat your barbecue (traditionally charcoal is used) for direct grilling on medium heat and barbecue the fish for 15 minutes, depending on its size, turning only once. To check if the wings are cooked, pierce with a long skewer and if it passes through with little resistance then remove from the heat and rest for a further 2 minutes to ensure the fish is cooked.

Serve the fish in the banana leaf, garnished with the onion, coriander and lime wedges.

CAPE TOWN
KINGFISH
FILLETS

I spent four months living in Cape Town, and I fell in love with the place. I couldn't believe the physical and spiritual energy of the Atlantic Ocean, poised at the point where it collides with such force into the Indian Ocean; the awesome surf and the insidious presence of every surfer's worst nightmare, the great white shark.

I remember cooking a meal for some Aussie mates in a wonderful cottage overlooking First Beach near Camps Bay. It was the first time I had ever cooked kingfish on the barbecue and it was sensational.

Kingfish is an oily, dark-fleshed fish, a little like tuna. It is highly prized as a sashimi fish and is high in natural fats such as omega 3 and 6. When chargrilled over a high heat and cooked medium, it is even better than tuna in my book. Watch it though, as overcooking has the tendency to dry it out. Try to buy fillets that are a similar size so they'll cook in the same amount of time. They'll go brilliantly with Anchovy and rosemary sauce (page 261).

Prepare your barbecue for direct grilling over a high heat. Ensure that the grill is clean and oil free.

Season the fish well with pepper and salt.

Place the fillets skin side down on the barbecue and cook for 5 minutes (for thick fillets). Turn over and cook for 2–3 minutes.

Remove from the grill to serving plates and allow to rest. For medium–rare, the fillets should be flaking on the outer part of the meat, and just undercooked or translucent in the centre.

SERVES 6

6 large (250 g) kingfish fillets

freshly ground black pepper

sea salt crystals or fine rock salt

KIWI BARBECUED
TROUT
WITH FIGS

SERVES 6

8 kaffir lime leaves

1 whole trout (2 kg) or small salmon,
cut into two fillets and pin-boned

3 limes

4 ripe figs, thickly sliced

1 tablespoon soft brown sugar

1 cup roughly chopped mint

1 cup roughly chopped flat-leaf parsley

¼ cup toasted pine nuts

sea salt

freshly cracked black pepper

extra lime wedges

Mark Gardner, the Kiwi chef I worked with on Surfing the Menu, cooked this recipe in the show. I made a joke about him using feijoas (the national fruit of New Zealand — they are awful!), so I have taken his recipe and swapped them for figs, a fruit that other people in the world will eat. One thing though: you'll need to use New Zealand trout because it's the only place that produces them big enough for this recipe. You'll also need to have butcher's string on hand.

As this dish is such a fantastic statement of what Kiwi food is all about — fresh and exciting combinations of flavours — I suggest that you serve the trout with Baked sweet potatoes with speck, cloves and maple syrup (page 55), washed down with a Southern Cross Pimm's (page 254), to maintain the theme.

Cut four lengths of butcher's string, making sure they are long enough to tie around the fish, and line them up, evenly spaced. Position a lime leaf in the centre of each piece of string, then place one fish fillet on top, skin side down. Make sure all the bones have been removed, then squeeze the juice of 1 lime over the flesh.

Place slices of fig along the fillet, dust with brown sugar and squeeze on some more lime juice. Sprinkle over the chopped herbs, followed by the pine nuts, and season with salt and pepper.

Place the remaining fillet on top of the seasoned fish and tie the string firmly. Slip the remaining lime leaves under the string, and season well with salt and pepper.

Prepare your barbecue for direct grilling over a medium–high heat.

Cook the fish for 6–8 minutes, then turn and cook for a further 5–6 minutes.

Allow to rest and serve with lime wedges.

SINGAPORE CHILLI CRABS

I came up with this version of Singapore chilli crab while I was holidaying in Port Douglas, in Far North Queensland. We'd met a couple at the apartments we were staying in, and Glen and I chartered a boat to go fishing. It cost us $120 each for the services of a guide who was more interested in making sure his missus dropped off a change of clothes for him so he could spend the night at the pub that evening!

One mud crab, a reef shark and three hours later, we returned triumphantly with the most expensive shark steaks and mud crab you could imagine. Bearing this in mind, along with the fact that it was Glen's birthday, I thought I'd give the crab the royal treatment. What really helped this recipe was the local sambal I bought at the markets. To replace it you could buy a commercial chilli sauce, but sambal is nice and salty so try to source some from a good Asian food store.

Preheat your barbecue hotplate to medium–high.

Place the prepared crabs in a large stainless steel bowl, along with the spring onion whites, the ketchup, sambal, peppers, ginger and garlic.

Pour the oil onto the hotplate, then add the contents of the bowl. Toss and fry.

Place the bowl over the crabs, then pour beer around the edge of the bowl so it seeps underneath and steams the crabs. Lift up the bowl and toss the crabs to ensure they cook evenly. If necessary, add more beer to continue steaming.

Remove the cover to check how they're going by breaking a section of crab. When the meat is white, they're cooked.

Season with salt and pepper, transfer to a serving dish and garnish with the spring onion greens and red chilli.

Serve straight away, with steamed rice.

SERVES 4

6 medium to large blue swimmer crabs, cleaned and halved, claws cracked

1 cup chopped spring onions, white part only, plus 1½ cups finely sliced spring onions, green tops only

250 ml (1 cup) tomato ketchup

1 tablespoon sambal

1–2 red Fire-roasted peppers (page 52), chopped

1 teaspoon chopped fresh ginger

1 teaspoon chopped garlic

100 ml sunflower oil

100 ml beer

salt

freshly ground black pepper

1 finely sliced red chilli

SQUID STUFFED WITH FENNEL AND BLACK PUDDING

SERVES 4

50 ml olive oil

1 large fennel bulb, finely diced

200 g Spanish blood sausage

salt

freshly ground black pepper

8 whole squid, tubes cleaned, tentacles trimmed and reserved

Fish and pork are a classic pairing, especially in this Spanish blend of crumbly morcilla (blood sausage) and squid. I think it's the spicy flavour and fat content of the sausage that works so well with the squid, and the addition of fennel gives a hint of aniseed to the dish. An alternative to stuffing the squid with the cooked fennel would be to serve the fennel as a shaved salad, with the addition of some mint.

Prepare your barbecue for direct grilling over a medium–high heat.

Gently fry the fennel in a little olive oil until soft, sweet and slightly golden. Allow to cool.

Remove the blood sausage from its outer skin and crumble onto the cooked fennel. Combine and season with salt and pepper.

Make lots of small cuts along the length of the tubes, to about 1 cm deep. This will allow the heat to penetrate the sausage, and it also looks impressive.

Stuff the squid tubes with the sausage and fennel mixture, being careful not to overfill them as the sausage will not heat through thoroughly when cooking. Reserve any left-over sausage mixture.

Once the tubes are stuffed, lightly oil and season the squid tubes. Place them cut-side down on the barbecue and cook for 3 minutes, until nicely charred. Turn over and cook for another 1–2 minutes. If you have any left-over sausage mixture, place it on the barbecue hotplate to cook at this point, along with the trimmed tentacles.

Serve the squid garnished with a sprinkling of any left-over cooked sausage and the cooked tentacles, with a light green salad.

BARBECUED
CRISPY-SKIN
KING SALMON

This recipe is great for serving on a large platter and sharing. I recently visited a salmon farm in the Marlborough region of New Zealand, where we cooked a whole side of the most amazing king salmon and served it with a simple salad. We pretty much devoured that salmon with our hands. (Well that's how chefs eat, generally — like animals!)

This recipe works well with a whole piece of salmon. You can use portions of salmon — just make sure the portions are cut from the middle of the fillet and are the same size.

Prepare your barbecue for direct cooking on a high heat. For this recipe I use the resting rack, so the fish is further from the heat source.

Blend all the avocado puree ingredients together and refrigerate until required.

For the salad, combine the shallots, radishes, apple, watercress and dill. Set aside.

Season the salmon with the lime juice, salt and pepper.

Place the fish on a strip of baking paper, skin side down, then place on the barbecue resting rack.

Close the hood and cook for about 8 minutes. Turn the fillet over and cook for another 8 minutes. Transfer the salmon to a large platter.

Remove the skin from the salmon and place the skin back on the resting rack. Close the hood — we want to get the skin really crispy.

Separate the salmon into large flakes — it should be just pink and moist. Dollop the avocado puree on the platter, in the gaps between the salmon.

Dress the salad with the oil, salt and pepper. Scatter it over the salmon and avocado puree.

Finally, remove the crisp skin from the barbecue and break it up over the salad. Serve straight away.

SERVES 4–6

750 g piece of salmon, cut from the thick middle of the fillet, skin on

juice of 1 lime

salt

ground white pepper

AVOCADO PUREE

1 avocado, peeled and stoned

3 tablespoons sour cream

1 teaspoon creamed horseradish

salt

ground white pepper

SALAD

2 shallots, thinly sliced into rings

5 breakfast radishes, finely sliced

½ apple, cut into thin matchsticks

1 punnet (about 100 g) of watercress, picked

2 tablespoons dill

1 tablespoon lime-infused macadamia oil

salt

freshly ground black pepper

BARBECUED
OYSTERS
WITH XO SAUCE, GINGER AND SHALLOT

24 large un-shucked Pacific oysters, shells washed

¼ cup finely julienned fresh ginger

¼ cup finely sliced spring onion greens

2 limes, cut into wedges

DRESSING

2 tablespoons XO sauce

2 tablespoons shaoxing rice wine

1 tablespoon light soy sauce

I love barbecued oysters. They're so easy, and perfect for grazing on while socialising. Bigger oysters, such as Pacific oysters, work best on the barbecue as they don't shrink too much. You do need to have un-shucked oysters for this recipe.

You'll find XO sauce in Chinese food stores and some delis — it's great stuff.

Prepare your barbecue for direct grilling over a high heat.

Combine the dressing ingredients in a small bowl.

Ensure your oysters are clean. Place the oyster shells between the barbecue grill bars, resting them so they stay upright.

As the oysters pop open, remove them to a tray that has been lined with scrunched-up foil.

Use a knife to prise open and remove the lid from the oysters, trying not to spill the juices. Loosen the oysters from the bottom shell with the tip of a sharp knife for ease of eating, so the oyster slides out of the shell, and dress each with a teaspoon of the dressing.

Garnish with a sprinkling of ginger and spring onion. Serve straight away, with the lime wedges.

MEAT

AUSSIE STEAK SANDWICH

SATAY SKEWERS

BEEF BRISKET TEXAS-STYLE

MEXICAN SUCKLING PIG TORTILLAS

PORK LOIN WITH BAY LEAVES
AND BALSAMIC

BARBECUED RIB OF BEEF

CLASSIC BARBECUED STICKY RIBS

LAMB KOFTE

LAMB BURGERS

THAI BEEF SALAD

LAMB SHISH WITH CHERMOULA

TANDOORI CHICKEN

JERKED CHICKEN

PERI-PERI CHICKEN

DAEGI BULGOGI: SPICY KOREAN PORK

BEST EVER CRISPY ROAST PORK BELLY

BARBECUED PEPPER CHICKEN CURRY

BENDER'S BEER-CAN CHICKEN

DAEGI GALBI: KOREAN PORK CUTLETS

CHAR SIU DUCK

PAMPLONA CHICKEN

CHAR SIU PORK

CHORIZO ROLL FROM BOROUGH MARKET

BISTECCA ALLA FIORENTINA

BARBECUED BUTTER CHICKEN TIKKA

BARBECUED BEEF IN BETEL LEAVES

BARBECUED SPICED QUAIL

BENDER'S DOUBLE CHEESE BURGER

CHINESE LACQUERED PORK BELLY

PULLED PORK SLIDER

BALINESE BARBECUED DUCK

KOREAN PORK WRAPS

DUKKAH-CRUSTED LAMB CUTLETS

LAMB SPARE RIBS

LEMONGRASS CHICKEN WINGS

BULGOGI: KOREAN BARBECUED BEEF

GRILLED RABBIT TRAPANI-STYLE

**LEMONGRASS AND TURMERIC
PORK RIB CUTLETS**

SPICED SMOKED CHICKEN

**GAI YANG: THAI BARBECUED
CHICKEN**

VIETNAMESE GRILLED BEEF

TIKKA LAMB CUTLETS

SMOKED BEEF SHORT RIBS WITH
NAM PRI PLA

ARGENTINEAN ASADO

In the early part of the twentieth century, Argentina produced grain and beef of the highest quality, so it's not too much of a surprise that Argentineans continue to consume a lot of meat.

An asado is a very popular, traditional method of cooking meat, originating in the Pampas regions of Argentina, Uruguay, Chile and Brazil. Typically, a wood fire burning on the ground or in a pit is surrounded by metal cross-stakes upon which the meat is rested, splayed open to receive the heat. The preparation is simple: the meat is merely seasoned with salt before and during the cooking process. It's a slow method of cooking, and the heat and the meat's distance from the fire need to be controlled. The meat juices and fat are never allowed to hit the fire because the smoke will affect the flavour of the meat, and often the fire is cleared from underneath the meat during the proceedings. The meat is generally transferred to a tray and typically served with chimichurri, a herb dressing.

Meat served at an asado is eaten in the following sequence: morcillas (blood sausages), chorizos, chinchulines (intestines), mollejas (sweetbreads) and other organs, followed by the ribs and steaks. Food cooked à la asado is when a parrilla (grill) is placed over coals that have formed from the fire and the meat is then cooked over the slow heat of the coals.

One of my kitchen porters used to reminisce about the asados back home in South America. They would build a big fire on the beach and skewer a whole strip loin on a star picket and then knock it into the ground next to the fire. As the fire burnt down they would move the star picket and the meat closer in until it was cooked. Now that's a barbecue!

SOUTH AMERICAN CHURRASCO

Churrasco is a Spanish/Portuguese word that defines the grilling of meat over a wood or coal fire. The definition varies across South America, from Central American countries such as Nicaragua, where it is used to describe long strips of tenderloin beef cooked on skewers and served with chimichurri, to Argentina, where it describes a large cut of beef that forms one of the courses cooked on an asado.

The true identity of the churrasco finds its origins in the southern regions of Brazil, where the gauchos (cowboys) of the Pampas regions would cook their meat over coals on spikes, as opposed to the grills found in Argentina and Uruguay. This style of cooking found its way via highway eateries and truck stops to the large cities, where the cooking technique became more sophisticated. Typically, the meat is not marinated but simply seasoned with a paste of salt and water brushed onto the meat as it cooks. It really is flame-cooked meat at its purest!

HOW TO COOK THE PERFECT STEAK

Most barbecue lovers are meat junkies, so it stands to reason that most barbecues involve cooking the odd steak. I know there are some criminal meat cooks out there, as I have witnessed some major acts of steak slaughter.

Follow these simple steps and you're guaranteed to end up with the perfect steak every time. It's worth remembering though that the quality of the meat is a huge factor in the tenderness and tastiness of the end product.

The selection of the right cut is important, as you're going to need a cut that is tender. The cuts that are best suited to the high heat of direct grilling are of course a well-marinated skirt steak or cuts such as sirloin, porterhouse, T-bone, rump or tenderloin (fillet). All these cuts have a broad surface area that takes advantage of the charred flavour from the high heat.

I recommend that the steaks be allowed to return to room temperature prior to grilling. This not only makes the cooking time shorter but also means that you lose less moisture from your meat.

Season your steaks just prior to grilling with coarsely ground rock salt or quality crystal salt and freshly ground pepper, or with spices if that's what you're using. If added early on, salt will draw moisture from the protein of the meat, which will in turn dissolve the salt. The coarse salt helps to protect the meat from sticking to the grill and also gives a lovely crust to the meat.

Your fire should be built or the gas arranged so you have a hot area and a cooler area so you can move your steak from the high heat to a more steady, lower heat. This is more important if you're cooking large, thick steaks as opposed to thin, quick-cook steaks. Be sure that your grill is clean and free of oil and fat, as they will impart a tainted flavour to your grilled meat. I never oil the steaks or the grill as oil cooking over a high heat will burn and flavour the meat. A hot fire and some seasoning are all you need to stop the steak from sticking.

Now it's time to cook your steaks. The golden rule is to never overcrowd your grill, as too many steaks will absorb the heat and lower the cooking temperature of the grill, especially if you're cooking on gas. Arrange your steaks in a row, in the order in which you plan to cook them. Organisation is the key to grill control.

Allow your steak to seal on the first side for 2–3 minutes, then rotate it 90 degrees so you end up with crisscross grill marks for presentation. You should only turn steaks a maximum of three times (this was something I was taught from a young age as a grill chef). Moisture from the steak will push up through the meat away from the heat. The trick is to create a balance between the two sides of the meat. Heat seals the meat surface, reducing the moisture's chance of escaping. If you allow the steak to remain on one side for too long, all the moisture will push out the other side and you will have a dry steak.

As a general rule, when cooking inch-thick steaks, turn them over after about 5 minutes and repeat the crisscross cooking on the other side. You will require a little less time on the second side, as the meat will be hotter; allow 3–4 minutes. Give the meat a final turn for just 30 seconds, just to heat the other side once again and to balance the movement of moisture.

To tell how cooked your steak is, the best method is to touch it. You should never cut a steak to check this. I use the finger to thumb method, which replicates the feeling of 'done-ness'. To do this feel the fleshy pad at the base of your thumb which should feel different depending on which finger is gently meeting your thumb. As a rough gauge; thumb and index finger = rare to medium–rare; thumb to middle finger = medium–rare to medium; thumb to ring finger = medium to medium-well-done; thumb to pinkie = medium-well-done to well-done.

The last step is the most important: the resting of the meat. When you cook meat, the protein contracts and the moisture heats up and moves from areas of high heat to lower heat (osmosis). Resting the meat after cooking allows the meat proteins to relax and the moisture that was moving outwards to return and settle within the meat. Rest the meat for half the time you took to cook it.

AUSSIE
STEAK
SANDWICH

SERVES 6

1 kg skirt or flank steak, trimmed of sinew, but leave the fat

12 pide (Turkish bread) pieces, split in half lengthways

2 vine-ripened tomatoes, sliced

2 handfuls rocket

MARINADE

2 garlic cloves, crushed

2 long red chillies

250 ml (1 cup) olive oil

2 tablespoons sherry vinegar

2 tablespoons worcestershire sauce

1 tablespoon tinned chopped tomatoes

100 ml kecap manis

1 teaspoon freshly ground black pepper

2 tablespoons thyme

ONION CONFIT

75 g butter

5 large onions, finely sliced

1 tablespoon sugar

1 rosemary sprig

HONEY–MUSTARD MAYONNAISE

4 tablespoons Mayonnaise (page 272)

1 tablespoon dijon mustard

2 teaspoons runny honey

Flank steak is an often-overlooked option when it comes to barbecuing. Cut from the belly, it is substantially tougher than rump or sirloin and benefits from being marinated and tenderised. Ideally, this recipe should marinate for two days. For this reason it has a far better flavour than most grilling steaks.

Flank steak is popular in France, where it is known as bavette, and also in Mexico, where it's called arrachera and is used in tortillas, and in Texas, where it is cooked slowly, like you would a brisket. I prefer the good old Aussie way! Marinate it really well and then just show it the fire. Cook it quickly and cut it thin, and you will enjoy the best steak sandwich this side of the black stump.

Prepare the marinade by combining all the ingredients in a food processor and blitzing. Rub into the trimmed steak and leave to marinate in the refrigerator overnight, but for the best flavour for 2 days.

Prepare the onion confit by melting the butter over a low heat. Add the onions, sugar and rosemary, and cook slowly until soft, golden and sweet. The confit can be made in advance and will keep for 1 month in the refrigerator if stored in an airtight container.

To make the honey–mustard mayo, simply combine all ingredients well.

Remove the meat from the marinade, pat it dry and allow to come to room temperature.

Prepare your barbecue for direct grilling over a high heat. I recommend that you cook the steak to medium-rare and no more (see page 141). Once cooked, allow the steak to rest.

Place the marinade in a small saucepan and cook until reduced.

Toast the bread slices on the grill on one side only, so you get crunch but not dryness.

To make each steak sandwich, spread the untoasted side of the bread with onion confit, add tomato and rocket, and dress with the mayonnaise. Slice the meat thinly, dress with the reduced marinade, place on top of your salad and top with a slice of toasted bread.

SATAY
SKEWERS

Grilling over hot coals is the only way to cook satay. It's best to cut the meat small, so you can put more on the sticks and it cooks through more quickly! The satay skewers are normally eaten on their own, but you could serve them with steamed rice and sliced cucumber.

I have a proper satay cooker in which I place pre-lit charcoal, then suspend the skewers over the heat, turning them often. If you don't have a satay cooker, prepare your barbecue for direct grilling on a medium heat. I suggest using just the front edge of the barbecue so that your meat and none of the sticks are exposed to the flame.

Puree all the marinade ingredients in a blender. Transfer to a bowl, then mix the meat through until well coated. Cover and marinate in the refrigerator overnight for best results.

Thread 6–8 pieces of meat up one end of each soaked bamboo skewer, leaving the other end of the skewer free. Discard any remaing marinade left in the bowl.

Pound the thicker end of a trimmed lemongrass stalk to make a brush for basting.

Place the skewers directly on the barbecue, or on a rack over the charcoal grill so only the meat is in contact with the heat. This will stop the bamboo skewers from burning.

Brush the satay with coconut milk while grilling. Cook, turning the satays frequently, for about 10 minutes – the meat will stay moist from the coconut milk and the natural fats from the meat.

Serve straight away, with Satay sauce and chopped coriander.

SERVES 10–12

2 kg chicken thighs, pork shoulder or thighs, cut into 1–2 cm cubes

Satay sauce (page 259), to serve

coconut milk, for brushing

chopped coriander

MARINADE

1 tablespoon ground coriander

1 tablespoon ground cumin

1 tablespoon Chinese five-spice

1 teaspoon ground turmeric

4 lemongrass stems, white part only (reserve one top to use as a brush)

1 garlic clove

3 tablespoons sugar

1 teaspoon tamarind juice or lemon juice

BEEF
BRISKET
TEXAS-STYLE

3 kg untrimmed brisket, the fattier the better

250 ml (1 cup) beer or water

RUB

1 tablespoon rock salt

3 tablespoons soft brown sugar

1 teaspoon crushed dried chillies

½ teaspoon Chinese five-spice

There are two schools of barbecuing in the US: east of the Mississippi, pork is the rock'n'roll of barbecues, while in Texas it's all about beef. This is a pretty straight-up recipe — just stick the meat in a bun with some delicious Coleslaw (page 74) and Basic barbecue sauce (page 258).

You'll need to have half a dozen cups of woodchips on hand for this recipe.

Combine the rub ingredients in a bowl.

Trim the brisket of any dry and unclean parts of meat. Cut the fat with a sharp knife in a crisscross fashion to allow the fat to render down and also so the rub can penetrate.

Rub the brisket with the sugar mix and leave to marinate in the refrigerator overnight.

Remove the brisket from the refrigerator and allow it to come to room temperature.

Now, the big job is getting the fire right. Whether you're using coals or gas, make sure you have enough fuel! Prepare your barbecue for indirect cooking over a medium–low heat, adding a handful of coals every hour to maintain the heat. Place the brisket in a roasting tray, fat side up, in the centre of the barbecue, away from any direct heat. If the fire is initially too hot, pour on a little beer or water into the tray to prevent any burning and also to help maintain the moisture in the brisket. Add ½ cup of pre-soaked hickory or mesquite chips to each side of the coals and pull down the hood on the barbecue. Now you just need to maintain the heat and add some woodchips each time you replenish the coals.

If using a gas barbecue, light the outer gas burners. Heat some pre-soaked woodchips in a smoke box prior to adding the brisket with the gas on high; when the woodchips start to smoke, turn the heat down, place the brisket on the grill racks between the gas burners and cook on a medium–low heat.

Cook the brisket for about 5 hours, basting with the tray juices until the meat is nice and tender and flakes under a fork. Once cooked, you can pull the meat or thinly slice it.

Pour the tray juices over the meat and serve.

MEXICAN
SUCKLING PIG
TORTILLAS

SERVES 10

1 suckling pig, or small pork shoulder on the bone (4–5 kg), lightly scored (ask your butcher to do this)

20 Tortillas (page 36)

2 quantities Guacamole (page 266)

2 quantities Shallot and coriander salsa (page 266)

1 quantity Refried beans (page 51)

500 g sour cream

1 quantity Mexican spicy green sauce (page 269)

ADOBO MARINADE

3 chipotle chillies, stems removed, soaked in hot water for 10 minutes

1 teaspoon smoked paprika

250 ml (1 cup) orange juice, or 125 ml (½ cup) grapefruit juice and 125 ml (½ cup) lime juice

60 ml (¼ cup) tomato ketchup

2 tablespoons dried wild oregano

½ teaspoon ground cumin

2 tablespoons white wine vinegar

2 teaspoons salt

½ teaspoon freshly ground black pepper

This is my all-time, pull-out-all-the-stops barbecue favourite. You have to get organised for this one, and you'll need a large barbecue. To make it easier, you could buy rather than make your tortillas. If you can't get hold of a suckling pig, use a shoulder from a younger animal.

Putting on a barbecue like this will have your friends and family talking about it for decades! I like to use habanero chillies (or use six regular chillies if you prefer), and I marinate the pork in a classic Mexican adobo marinade — it goes well with fish or chicken too, but with pork it rocks!

Place all the marinade ingredients in a food processor and blitz. Place the mix in a large plastic bag, along with the pork. Extract as much air as you can and tie the bag closed. Leave to marinate in the refrigerator for at least 4–5 hours.

Remove the pork from the refrigerator and allow it to come to room temperature.

Set up a large hooded barbecue with a spit. If you don't have a spit, prepare your barbecue for indirect cooking, starting at a relatively high heat. Pour 500 ml (2 cups) water into the drip tray underneath the grill, to help maintain moisture within the barbecue, and keep topping it up as you cook. If using a gas barbecue, place a wire rack over a large roasting tray and add 500 ml (2 cups) water to the tray. Turn on the outer gas burners for indirect cooking.

Place the pork on the grill racks, put the lid on the barbecue and cook at a medium–high temperature for 30 minutes, then lift the lid to cool. Cook for 4–5 hours with the lid down, basting with the left-over marinade from time to time. Maintain the heat at a medium–low level by adding coals every 30–40 minutes.

Once the pork is tender, remove to a large tray or board to rest. Fire up the coals while this is happening so you can heat your tortillas.

Carve the meat and serve in tortillas topped with guacamole, salsa, refried beans, sour cream and spicy green sauce.

PORK LOIN
WITH BAY LEAVES
AND BALSAMIC

The ancient Romans used to honour their heroes with wreaths of laurel leaves, so I am honouring the mighty pig with a barbecue and bay leaves! We used to make this dish at the River Café using top-quality rare-breed pork. I doubt you will find a better recipe.

The pork loin goes really well with Baked beans (page 50), mixed with a handful of rocket.

Combine the garlic, rosemary, bay leaves, vinegar and oil.

Score the fat of the pork loin with a sharp knife in a crisscross fashion and season with black pepper.

Pour over the balsamic and olive oil mixture and leave to marinate for 2–3 hours at room temperature.

Prepare your barbecue for indirect cooking, although we will be using a direct grilling method to seal and colour the pork.

Cook the pork loin over direct medium–high heat, allowing the fat to caramelise and blacken slightly. Transfer to a lower indirect heat and cook, covered, for 25–30 minutes in a roasting or foil tray with a little of the marinade (make sure you include the rosemary and bay leaves).

Place the remaining marinade in a small saucepan and cook until reduced.

Serve the pork drizzled with the reduced marinade.

SERVES 4

4 garlic cloves, chopped

1 rosemary sprig, roughly chopped

8 fresh bay leaves

150 ml balsamic vinegar

60 ml (¼ cup) olive oil

2–2.5 kg pork loin

1 teaspoon freshly cracked black pepper

BARBECUED
RIB OF BEEF

I've always enjoyed cooking large pieces of meat over coals — I suppose it's the closest I get to cooking gaucho-style. The cowboys of the Pampas regions of South America are the masters of this style of cooking, impaling large joints of meat and roasting them on an open fire.

This recipe is best followed using an indirect heating method: prepare your coals on one side of your barbecue, or if you have a gas grill pull down the hood, turn your middle gas burners off and crank up the outer gas burners. Add some pre-soaked woodchips for extra flavour.

You'll need to make a brush from lightly bruised sprigs of thyme and rosemary tied together, and use it to brush the ribs with the British beef wash.

If using coals, prepare your barbecue for indirect cooking well in advance so you build up a good heat base. Whether you're using coals or gas, pour a little water into the drip tray underneath the grill to help maintain moisture within the barbecue; you'll need to top it up from time to time.

While the barbecue is heating up, take the rib of beef out of the refrigerator and allow it to come to room temperature. This will help ensure it cooks evenly.

To make the British beef wash, place all the ingredients in a jar and shake to combine. Brush the rib roast with the wash, and give it another good brushing before you start cooking.

Place the beef on the barbecue while it is at its hottest and cover with the hood or lid of the barbecue. After the initial burst of heat (about 15–20 minutes), allow the coals to ease in intensity and maintain this heat by adding a few coals from time to time, along with some pre-soaked woodchips for smoke. If using a gas barbecue, turn the gas down slightly to maintain a medium heat. Add a handful of pre-soaked woodchips to the smoke box from time to time to maintain a gentle smoke.

Brush the rib roast liberally with the beef wash at intervals.

A joint of this size will take 1½–2 hours to cook. Allow the fire to burn down during the last 30 minutes of cooking time. At this stage, prepare the barbecue sauce to glaze the beef.

Allow the beef to rest for 20 minutes, then carve, glazing with the sauce.

SERVES 6

3 kg rib roast, with 6–8 bones; ask your butcher to cut off the chin and backbone, leaving just the rib bones

80 ml (⅓ cup) Basic barbecue sauce (page 258)

BRITISH BEEF WASH

1 tablespoon hot water

1 tablespoon salt

2 tablespoons sherry vinegar

1 tablespoon English mustard

2 tablespoons worcestershire sauce

CLASSIC
BARBECUED
STICKY RIBS

SERVES 4–6

3–4 kg pork baby back ribs

250 ml (1 cup) apple juice

RUB

1 teaspoon Celery salt (page 279)

1 tablespoon soft brown sugar

1 tablespoon salt

1 teaspoon chilli powder

1 teaspoon smoked paprika

1 teaspoon freshly cracked black pepper

1 teaspoon mustard powder

1 tablespoon onion flakes

1 tablespoon garlic flakes

GLAZE

1 cup brown sugar

250 ml (1 cup) malt vinegar

½ cinnamon stick

1 small dried red chilli, crumbled

250 ml (1 cup) tomato ketchup

1 tablespoon dijon mustard

100 g creamed horseradish

100 ml dark rum

Barbecued ribs conjure up images of classic American barbecues. They're slow-cooked, to achieve meat that's tender, moist and smoky, and finished with a sticky-sweet, sometimes sharp sauce or glaze.

There are thousands of recipes for these babies — there are even world barbecue championships to find the best rib recipes! Some people boil their ribs first, but true practitioners of the fine art of barbecuing believe this is a cardinal sin. The only way to achieve perfection is firstly to rub the ribs and then to barbecue them. The rub is generally a mix of salt, sugar and spices, which cures the meat, drawing out excess moisture and concentrating the flavour. The sugar helps to tenderise the flesh and slowly caramelises during the barbecue process to add to the wonderful flavour of the meat. You will need about 6–8 handfuls of soaked woodchips for this one.

Make the rub by placing the ingredients in a food processor and mixing until fine. Rub over the pork ribs and leave to marinate in the refrigerator for 2–3 hours or overnight. The rub will keep for 1 month if stored in an airtight container, but you should use it all in this recipe.

Remove the ribs from the refrigerator and allow them to come to room temperature.

Prepare your barbecue for indirect cooking over low–medium heat (roughly 100–120°C if you have a thermometer). Add a handful of pre-soaked woodchips to the coals, place the ribs over a drip tray and cook with the lid on until soft and tender, or until the bone pulls away from the meat. This will take 2–3 hours to do properly. Add woodchips every 40 minutes or so to keep the gentle smoke flavour going.

If using a gas barbecue, light the outer gas burners. Heat some pre-soaked woodchips in a smoke box prior to adding the ribs with the gas on high; when the woodchips start to smoke, turn the heat down, place the ribs on the grill racks between the gas burners and cook on a low–medium heat as above.

Spray the ribs with apple juice from time to time to keep them moist.

While the ribs are cooking, combine the glaze ingredients in a saucepan and bring to the boil. Simmer until thick then keep warm.

Once the ribs are cooked, cut them between the bones and place in a dish. Toss through the glaze then return the ribs to the barbecue, this time over direct heat to get them nice and hot and sticky.

Transfer to a serving dish and eat straight away.

LAMB
KOFTE

KOFTE

500 g lean lamb, finely minced

2 tablespoons chopped sweet marjoram or oregano

4 tablespoons chopped flat-leaf parsley

4 chopped spring onions

1 teaspoon ground cumin

salt

freshly ground black pepper

1 egg, beaten

TO SERVE

5 flatbreads

good-quality hummus

Tabouleh (page 88), to serve

1 quantity Minted yoghurt
(next page; from the Lamb burgers recipe)

5 tablespoons Harissa (page 262)

Throughout North Africa and the Middle East, kofte generally refers to lamb mince, either in meatball form or squashed by hand onto long skewers and cooked over braziers. I have encountered other meat varieties such as camel and beef, but more often than not it is lamb.

Some of my fondest memories of travelling through Morocco are of the souk stallholders busily cooking over charcoal braziers, the smell and the hectic atmosphere as disorienting as they were inspiring. The Djemma el Fna, a massive square in Marrakech, is just about the best street food market in the world.

I got this recipe from a butcher in Casablanca, merely by observation, and you can use it however you wish. I like to make big lamb burgers using kofte, so I've included the recipe here. I would serve the kofte in wraps instead of buns though.

You can also use the mixture to make Lamb burgers (page 155).

Combine the lamb with the herbs, spring onions, cumin, salt and pepper. Mix together really well.

Add the beaten egg and combine with a wooden spoon until the egg is completely incorporated. Leave to rest for 30 minutes.

Take small balls of the lamb mixture and squeeze them onto 10 metal skewers, into long sausage shapes.

Cook over hot coals without a grill rack until well browned all over and cooked through.

Lightly toast the flatbreads on one side and spread the untoasted side with hummus. Add some tabouleh, then place two kofte on each. Top with the minted yoghurt and harissa, roll up and serve straight away.

LAMB
BURGERS

Prepare your barbecue for direct grilling over a medium–high heat.

Place the patties on the barbecue and cook on one side, without moving, for 6–8 minutes. Make sure they set and don't crumble; if you try to move them too soon they will fall apart. Turn the patties over and cook for a further 5–8 minutes. You want them to be well cooked; as with any minced or processed product, the chances of food poisoning are greater than with whole cuts of meat.

Make the minted yoghurt by stirring the chopped mint through the yoghurt and seasoning with salt and pepper.

Toss the lettuce with the coriander, dress with the lemon juice and season with salt and pepper.

Toast one side of the buns. Top the untoasted side with the dressed lettuce, tomato and a burger. Add a good dollop of the minted yoghurt and harissa, top with the other half of the bun and serve straight away.

SERVES 5

1 quantity Lamb kofte (previous page), formed into 5 patties

1 cos lettuce, chopped

1 bunch coriander, leaves picked

juice of 1 lemon

salt

freshly ground black pepper

5 burger buns, split lengthways

3 tomatoes, sliced

5 tablespoons Harissa (page 262)

MINTED YOGHURT

½ bunch mint, leaves chopped

100 g plain yoghurt

salt

freshly ground black pepper

THAI
BEEF SALAD

When my wife Dee and I are watching what we eat, or we feel like eating something that makes us feel good about ourselves, this one's a no-brainer. It's the perfect detox treatment. I love the clean, fresh flavours, and the heat to get the heart pumping, plus it's so quick to put together.

The Thai people did not invent the barbecue but they've come up with some of the best barbecue recipes in the world. I nearly always save a couple of steaks for this salad so I can serve something a bit different when I put on a barbecue. It's ideal served with steamed rice to help cool things down.

Finely slice the spring onions on the diagonal and place in a bowl with the chillies, shallots, coriander and lemongrass.

Prepare your barbecue for direct grilling over a high heat. Season the beef with a good amount of salt and pepper, then cook to your liking. I prefer medium–well-done as I think you get a more flavourful salad. Allow the meat to rest while you dress the salad.

Squeeze the lime juice over the spring onion salad, followed by the fish sauce, then toss to combine. Slice the meat finely, removing the fat. Add to the salad, toss to combine the flavours and serve.

SERVES 4

2 bunches spring onions, washed, outer leaves removed, roots and tops trimmed

3 red chillies, finely sliced

10 red Asian shallots, finely sliced

1 bunch coriander, washed and chopped

3 lemongrass stems, white part only, thinly sliced

400 g rump or sirloin steak

salt

freshly ground black pepper

juice of 3 limes, or to taste

100 ml fish sauce

LAMB SHISH
WITH CHERMOULA

SERVES 6

500 g diced leg of lamb

6 flatbreads

6 tablespoons good-quality hummus

1 quantity Tabouleh (page 88)

olive oil

CHERMOULA MARINADE

3 tablespoons Harissa (page 262)

½ cup chopped flat-leaf parsley

½ cup chopped mint

½ cup chopped coriander leaves

2 garlic cloves, peeled

½ teaspoon ground cinnamon

½ teaspoon ground cumin

1 small lemon, roughly chopped, seeds removed

½ cup plain yoghurt

1 teaspoon sea salt

SPICED YOGHURT

1 cup plain yoghurt

½ teaspoon ground cumin

salt

freshly ground black pepper

Shish are generally skewers threaded with chunks of lamb or chicken, cooked over coals. I have seen Greek and Turkish barbecues where they have huge skewers that are turned over coals by an electric rotisserie, but not too many people would have one of them at home!

Long metal skewers are easy enough to find, and all you need to do is lift the meat away from the grill bars to get a flame-roasted effect. You can do this by placing two bricks at either end of the grill so you can suspend the skewers over the heat. If you have a kettle barbecue you could balance the skewers on the edge of the barbecue, if your skewers are long enough; if not, just use bricks.

Charcoal is by far the best method for this recipe.

Combine all the chermoula marinade ingredients in a large bowl. Toss the lamb in the marinade until thoroughly coated. Leave to marinate in the refrigerator overnight.

Remove the lamb from the refrigerator and allow it to come to room temperature. When ready to cook, thread the meat onto metal skewers and refrigerate while you prepare the charcoal for direct grilling over a high heat. If using a gas barbecue, crank it up to the highest setting.

Cook the skewers for as long as you desire — I prefer them to be cooked medium.

While the lamb shish is cooking, make the spiced yoghurt by combining the yoghurt with the cumin, salt and pepper.

Warm the flatbreads on the grill, then spread with the hummus and a large spoonful of tabouleh. Place the lamb on top and dress with the spiced yoghurt and olive oil.

Serve the bread open like a plate, or roll it up like a souvlaki.

TANDOORI
CHICKEN

Tandoori chicken has got to be one of the most instantly recognisable Indian dishes. The famously smoky marinated chicken is traditionally cooked in a terracotta tandoor oven over a charcoal fire.

The history of tandoor ovens reaches back over several thousands of years to Punjab in Pakistan. They are amazing ovens and can reach extreme temperatures. The high heat seals in the flavour and moisture, and imparts a lovely smokiness. Often the meat has a red appearance with touches of black, caused by the intense heat. The red is generally due to the use of red chillies in the marinade, although nowadays annatto, a red food colour, is added.

Tandoori chicken is traditionally served with sliced onion and lemon wedges, and also goes well with Spiced red bean salad (page 88).

Make deep cuts into the breast and thighs of the chicken, keeping the bird whole. Alternatively, you could cut through the backbone and flatten the bird with your hands.

Rub the chicken with the lemon juice, ginger, garlic and salt. Cover and leave to marinate in the refrigerator for 1 hour.

Combine the red marinade ingredients in a bowl. Coat the chicken with the marinade, then cover and refrigerate for a further 2 hours.

Remove the chicken from the refrigerator and allow it to come to room temperature.

Prepare your barbecue for indirect cooking over a high heat. Place the chicken away from the coals with a tray underneath the meat. Add ½ cup of pre-soaked woodchips to the coals and when they start to smoke, place the lid on the barbecue.

If using a gas barbecue, light the outer gas burners. Heat some pre-soaked woodchips in a smoke box prior to adding the chicken with the gas on high; when the woodchips start to smoke, turn the heat down, place the chicken on the grill racks between the gas burners and cook on a high heat.

Cook the chicken for 45–50 minutes. Maintain the heat at medium–high after the initial hot start, with the addition of a few extra coals to either side if you're using charcoal.

To serve, simply joint the chicken into four pieces.

SERVES 4

1.5 kg chicken, skinned and washed

juice of 1 lemon

1 cm piece fresh ginger, finely chopped

2 garlic cloves, crushed

salt

RED MARINADE

500 g Greek-style yoghurt

5 garlic cloves, crushed

3 cm piece fresh ginger, finely chopped

2 tablespoons sunflower oil

3 teaspoons garam masala

2 tablespoons lime juice

100 g red chilli paste

1 teaspoon salt

JERKED
CHICKEN

12 chicken thighs, bone in

chopped spring onions, to garnish

MARINADE

½ bunch spring onions, chopped

¼ bunch coriander, chopped

3 Scotch bonnet or other hot chillies

60 ml (¼ cup) tomato ketchup

2 tablespoons lime juice

1 tablespoon cider vinegar

1 tablespoon brown sugar

2 teaspoons thyme

1 cm piece fresh ginger, finely chopped

1½ teaspoons salt

1 teaspoon ground allspice or ground pimento

1 teaspoon freshly cracked black pepper

½ teaspoon ground nutmeg

½ teaspoon ground cinnamon

The word 'barbecue' originates in the Caribbean. The Taíno People of the Caribbean dug pits to cook their food, building fires overlaid with green branches of the pimento tree. The branches formed a rack on which the meat was then cooked.

Things have since moved on somewhat in the Caribbean, and these days it's more common to see barbecues made from old oil barrels cut in half (the same barrels from which they make kettle drums), over which their famous jerk meat is cooked. The thing that makes jerk so great is the use of the aromatic and super-hot Scotch bonnet chilli. Warning! Approach these chillies with caution.

Jerked chicken is great served with Caribbean rice and beans (page 57).

Trim the chicken thighs of any excess fat and skin. Wash and pat dry.

Combine the marinade ingredients in a food processor and blend until smooth.

Rub the marinade all over the chicken (you might like to wear disposable gloves to do this). Place the chicken in a plastic or ceramic dish. Marinate in the refrigerator for at least 3 hours, or overnight if possible.

Remove the chicken from the refrigerator and allow it to come to room temperature.

Prepare your barbecue for direct grilling. Have one side at a medium–high heat and around one-third of the heat source at a lower heat to allow the chicken to cook slowly, preventing the marinade from burning.

Initially, place the thighs over the higher heat to seal and colour the chicken. Add half a cup of pre-soaked woodchips to the lower heat source, then move the chicken to slowly cook over the lower heat for 15–20 minutes. If using gas, heat your woodchips in a smoke box prior to moving the chicken to cook over the lower heat.

Sprinkle with spring onions and serve while hot.

PERI-PERI
CHICKEN

Cooked with a touch of smokiness, I think this recipe is one of the best barbecue chicken dishes in the world. It has Portuguese roots and is common throughout Africa due to Portugal's colonial interests. Peri-peri is the name used for the African bird's eye chilli, and in marinades it usually refers to a beautiful blend of paprika and other spices, combined with the acidity of lime or vinegar. It doesn't have to be outrageously hot.

The peri-peri marinade will keep for up to a week if stored in an airtight container.

To make the marinade, place the chopped chillies and salt in a mortar or food processor and make a paste.

Add the garlic, ginger and spices, and pound or grind to a paste. Add the vinegar and oregano.

Make two or three slashes in each chicken thigh, cutting to the bone.

Add the chicken to the marinade. Marinate in the refrigerator overnight, or for a minimum of 3 hours.

Remove the chicken from the refrigerator and allow it to come to room temperature.

Prepare your barbecue for direct grilling over a medium heat. Barbecue the chicken thighs for 5–8 minutes, just to colour on each side, then remove from the heat. Wet your smoking herbs liberally and place them on the barbecue, arranging the chicken over the top. Continue to cook the chicken with the lid on until cooked through. This may take 20 minutes.

When cooked, drizzle the chicken with olive oil and serve with the lime wedges and a spoonful of aïoli.

SERVES 6

12 chicken thighs, bone in, trimmed of excess fat

2 tablespoons olive oil

3 limes, cut into wedges

1 quantity Aïoli (page 273)

PERI-PERI MARINADE

2–3 Scotch bonnet or other hot chillies, roughly chopped

4 long red chillies, roughly chopped

2 teaspoons sea salt

2 garlic cloves, crushed

5 cm piece fresh ginger, roughly chopped

2 teaspoons ground coriander

½ teaspoon ground cinnamon

1 teaspoon ground paprika

100 ml white wine vinegar

2 teaspoons chopped oregano

TO SMOKE

1 branch bay leaves

1 large bunch rosemary

1 large bunch curly or flat-leaf parsley

1 bunch thyme

1 bunch sage

DAEGI BULGOGI:
SPICY
KOREAN PORK

SERVES 6

500 g pork fillet, cut into thin strips

60 ml (¼ cup) soy sauce

5 garlic cloves, crushed

1 cm piece fresh ginger, finely chopped

2 tablespoons palm sugar
or light brown sugar

2 tablespoons kochujang

1 teaspoon chilli flakes

2 tablespoons rice wine

2 tablespoons sesame oil

sunflower oil

1 onion, finely sliced

½ iceberg lettuce

1 butterleaf or lollo rosso lettuce

60 ml (¼ cup) Ssamjang (page 268)

200 g Kimchi (page 81)

1 cup mint

This popular Korean dish is eaten in the same fashion as the barbecued Bulgogi (page 208), with lettuce wraps, herbs, kimchi and spicy ssamjang sauce. The pork is marinated in a red pepper sauce called kochujang, as well as ginger, soy, sesame oil, garlic and sugar. Daegi is Korean for pork and bulgogi means 'fire meat', so this dish is known as 'pork fire meat'.

I just love this style of grazing. Pork is just about the best meat to barbecue in the world, and the Koreans have nailed it with this number!

To make the bulgogi, combine the pork, soy sauce, garlic, ginger, sugar, kochujang, chilli flakes, rice wine and sesame oil. Leave to marinate in the refrigerator for at least 30 minutes, but no longer than 1 hour.

Remove the pork from the refrigerator and allow it to come to room temperature.

Heat your barbecue hotplate to medium—hot. Add a little sunflower oil to the hotplate and start to quickly fry the marinated meat. Add the onion and use a spatula to turn the meat. I like to cook the pork to medium, but most people prefer their pork well done.

Transfer the pork to a serving platter, along with the lettuce, ssamjang and kimchi.

To eat, take a lettuce leaf and add a little ssamjang, kimchi and pork, top with mint and roll up to make a wrap.

BEST EVER
CRISPY ROAST
PORK BELLY

This is a secret recipe given to me by a guy called Danny, who owns some restaurants in Darwin. (Sorry Danny, it's not a secret anymore!) This recipe works so well. You can use it as a starting point for myriad other pork dishes, or serve it with other sauces that will make it taste even better.

I like to serve the pork belly as a finger food on a large platter, garnished with a sprinkling of chilli and coriander.

Place your pork belly on a chopping board, skin side up. Using a skin pricker or a meat needle, puncture the skin repeatedly for about 5 minutes. (Don't be scared to use a bit of force — get angry!) Once you are satisfied with your acupuncture work, rub the skin of the belly well with the bicarbonate of soda.

Cover with a clean cloth and leave at room temperature for about 1 hour, so that the bicarbonate of soda can soak up the moisture from the skin.

Meanwhile, prepare your barbecue for indirect cooking over a low to medium heat (about 150°C maximum if you have a thermometer).

After 1 hour, use a wet cloth to wipe all the bicarbonate of soda from the skin of the pork. Wipe the skin dry with a clean cloth.

Place the pork belly on a roasting rack in a roasting tin and fill the bottom with water. Place on the barbecue. Cook for 2 hours with the hood down, until the pork is tender, adding water to the roasting tin if it starts to dry out.

Once you're happy with the tenderness of the pork — the skin should still be soft at this point, not crackly — remove it from the barbecue.

Raise the temperature to high heat, about 250°C. Drain most of the water from the tin and place the pork back on the barbecue still in the roasting tin. Keeping a close eye on proceedings, cook the pork until the skin puffs and crackles up. This is best done by observation as times will vary.

Once the skin is evenly crackled, remove the pork from the barbecue and leave to rest. (I like to remove the crackling in one sheet from the belly meat, trim off any excess fat and≈sprinkle the crackling well with salt.)

Cut the pork belly into cubes. Break up the crackling and arrange over the pork. Scatter with chilli and coriander and serve straight away.

SERVES 6

2 kg pork belly — 'medium fatty' is fine, but lean is not! (It's best in one portion for ease of pricking and cooking but 2 x 1 kg pieces work well enough)

3 tablespoons bicarbonate of soda

flaked salt

1 red chilli, thinly sliced

coriander, to garnish

BARBECUED
PEPPER CHICKEN
CURRY

SERVES 6

4 long fat green chillies

2 short hot green chillies

8 garlic cloves, peeled

sunflower oil

juice of 2 large lemons

2 teaspoons ground turmeric

1.6 kg chicken, jointed for sautéing, skin removed

1 teaspoon cumin seeds

2 onions, chopped

2 teaspoons crushed coriander seeds

2 teaspoons freshly cracked black pepper

12 fresh curry leaves

1 cup coriander chopped leaves

½ cucumber, chopped

100 g plain yoghurt

salt

freshly ground black pepper

This dish started out as a simple curry, but during England's summer festival season I was asked to put on a barbecue over fifteen nights at an open-air festival in Wimbledon. I needed to cook something with a big impact, something that would send out irresistible aromas, so I took this recipe and converted it for the barbecue. Man, it went down a treat!

The only thing you need is a flat griddle plate or you could use a large cast-iron pan on an open fire. It's absolutely fabulous with a cool yoghurt and cucumber dressing, Spiced red bean salad (page 88) or even with Whole pumpkin biryani (page 58).

Puree the chillies and garlic in a food processor, adding a little oil if necessary.

Place the chillies and garlic in a bowl with the lemon juice and turmeric. Add the jointed chicken and mix well. Leave to marinate in the refrigerator for a minimum of 2 hours.

Remove the chicken from the refrigerator and allow it to come to room temperature.

Preheat your barbecue hotplate to medium or place a flat griddle pan over the barbecue coals. Pour a little oil onto the barbecue hotplate and start to cook the chicken, turning it so the meat is evenly coloured. Allow the barbecue to burn down to a medium—low heat.

Pour a little more oil onto the hotplate and add the cumin seeds, onions, crushed coriander seeds and black pepper. Fry until the onions start to colour and the aromas of the spices begin to develop. Add the remaining marinade and curry leaves. Continue to cook, turning the chicken until cooked through; this could take 25 minutes in all.

When the chicken is cooked, add the coriander.

Combine the cucumber with the yoghurt and season with salt and pepper. Either drizzle the yoghurt mixture over the chicken, or serve it separately.

BENDER'S
BEER-CAN
CHICKEN

I don't know who thought up this wicked way of cooking a chicken, but I'm sure it started off as a joke. I have seen it done in both Australia and New Zealand. Obviously, the Kiwis will say that they did it first, and the thing is, they probably did. I like to use Japanese Sapporo beer for this recipe.

In his book *The Barbecue! Bible*, Grill Master Steve Raichlen writes that he got the inspiration for this technique while attending a world barbecue championship. I suppose everyone has their own method, but one thing I should point out is that you need to open the can of beer or you may find there's not much of your chicken left after the can explodes!

Trim the chicken of any excess fat from the neck end of the bird and the cavity. Remove any giblets. Fold the wing tips in so that they don't hang out.

Rub the chimichurri inside the chicken cavity and between the skin and the meat. Leave the bird to rest while you fire up the barbecue.

Set up your barbecue for indirect cooking, placing a foil tray under the grill.

Open the can of beer and drink a mouthful — just one big sip. Push the lemon quarters into the can of beer, along with the rosemary sprigs.

Push the can, open end first, into the chicken cavity. The trick is to balance the chicken so that it stands over the grill without falling over.

Cook, covered, for 1½ hours, adding charcoal as required to maintain an even, moderate heat.

The chicken is cooked when the juices run clean from an incision made in the thickest part of the bird, which is generally the thigh.

When cooked, carefully remove to a tray and allow to rest. Remember to discard the beer can before serving!

SERVES 6

1.8 kg chicken

2 tablespoons Chimichurri (page 264)

375 ml can wheat beer

1 lemon, cut into quarters

2 rosemary sprigs

DAEGI GALBI:
KOREAN
PORK CUTLETS

SERVES 6

10–12 streaky pork belly cutlets, skin removed, cutlets cut into strips 5 cm thick

MARINADE

2 onions, finely chopped

10 garlic cloves, crushed

2 cm piece fresh ginger, finely chopped

250 ml (1 cup) kochujang

4 tablespoons sugar

2 tablespoons soy sauce

60 ml (¼ cup) sesame oil

1 teaspoon freshly cracked black pepper

These spicy Korean pork cutlets rock! Koreans would usually use ribs, but I like to make this recipe using streaky pork cutlets cut from the belly, as you get more meat than bone, and a nice amount of fat adds to the lovely flavours.

The spice mixture is quite hot, due to the kochujang (red pepper sauce), so it's best served with Kimchi (page 81) on the side to help control the heat. Once you start eating these cutlets it's hard to stop, mainly because the chilli starts to kick in if you do!

Puree the marinade ingredients, then rub the marinade into the pork meat. Leave to marinate in the refrigerator for 4–5 hours, or overnight.

Remove the pork from the refrigerator and allow it to come to room temperature.

Prepare your barbecue for direct grilling over a medium–high heat. Cook the pork for 8–10 minutes on either side.

Serve straight away.

CHAR SIU
DUCK

SERVES 4

2 kg Muscovy or Chinese duck

CHAR SIU MARINADE

60 ml (¼ cup) honey

60 ml (¼ cup) dark soy sauce

1 teaspoon Chinese five-spice

2 garlic cloves, crushed

2 cm piece fresh ginger, finely chopped

2 tablespoons shaoxing rice wine or sherry

When I moved from Perth to Sydney at the age of twenty-one, it really opened my eyes. There were many things I'd never experienced. I will always remember my first trip to BBQ King in Chinatown, seeing the chefs hard at it and the rows of ducks hanging up, their ochre-coloured skin glistening from the glaze and drying to perfection. I have been trying to replicate the BBQ King chefs' efforts ever since, and love returning to the restaurant for the ultimate Chinese barbecue.

This dish is great served with steamed rice and Chinese greens. I suggest you cook two char siu ducks, as one is never enough!

To make the marinade, place the honey and soy sauce in a saucepan and bring to the boil. Remove from the heat, add the remaining ingredients and allow to stand until cold.

Cut the duck through the back and flatten it (your butcher could do this for you). Pour a kettleful of boiling water over the duck three times, draining each time. Pat the duck dry, place in the marinade and leave to marinate in the refrigerator overnight, turning once or twice.

Remove the duck from the refrigerator and allow it to come to room temperature. Drain and reserve the marinade.

Prepare your barbecue for indirect cooking over a medium heat. Pour 1 litre (4 cups) water into the drip tray underneath the grill, to help maintain moisture within the barbecue. If using a gas barbecue, place a wire rack over a large roasting tray and add 1 litre (4 cups) to the tray. Turn on the outer gas burners for indirect cooking.

Place the duck on the grill racks, put the lid on the barbecue and cook for around 1 hour. Maintain the heat at a medium level by adding a handful of preheated coals when necessary. If the edges start to blacken or darken too much, just rotate the duck or leave the lid ajar to lower the heat.

Boil the marinade in a saucepan and reduce to a thick glaze. Just prior to removing the duck from the barbecue, brush it with the glaze. Allow to rest for 10 minutes before serving.

PAMPLONA
CHICKEN

Uruguayans cook this fire-roasted dish with pork or chicken, as the cheese and roasted peppers work really well with both types of meat.

The combination of flavours here hints at various European influences. The smoked ham and cheese have a Germanic leaning, while provolone is an Italian speciality cheese, and the peppers are a staple at most Italian barbecues.

This chicken is best cooked on charcoal, and it's great served with Chimichurri (page 264) and Shaved fennel and celery salad (page 87).

Spread out the boned chicken, skin side down. Remove the breast fillets and arrange them on the breast skin. Season with salt, pepper and wild oregano.

Arrange the fire-roasted peppers over the chicken, followed by the cheese and smoked ham.

Roll up the chicken to form a fat Swiss roll, then secure with two or three pre-soaked wooden skewers. Rub the skin with olive oil and season with salt and pepper.

Set up your barbecue for direct grilling over a medium heat.

Place the chicken on the barbecue and cook for 20 minutes, turning frequently to prevent burning. Ensure that the heat is maintained at medium.

When cooked, allow to rest for 10 minutes before carving.

SERVES 4

1.5 kg chicken, boned flat (ask your butcher to do this)

salt

freshly ground black pepper

1 tablespoon dried wild oregano

3 Fire-roasted peppers (page 52)

5 slices provolone or mozzarella, 5 mm thick

100 g smoked ham, thinly sliced

olive oil

CHAR SIU
PORK

Most people would be familiar with the lovely red strips of pork or duck hanging in the windows of Cantonese restaurants in Chinatowns around the world. It really is quite an easy thing to make yourself, and it's fantastic with simple greens and steamed rice. I've eaten it in Hong Kong with fried eggs.

The pork neck in this recipe is a cut from the top portion of the shoulder. It's good for this dish as it has a reasonable fat content.

Cut the pork neck so it's a similar thickness all the way through (your butcher could do this for you). Immerse the pork in the cold marinade and leave to marinate in the refrigerator overnight, turning once or twice.

Remove the pork from the refrigerator and allow it to come to room temperature. Drain and reserve the marinade.

Prepare your barbecue for indirect cooking over a medium heat. Pour 1 litre (4 cups) water into the drip tray underneath the grill, to help maintain moisture within the barbecue, topping it up as you cook. If using a gas barbecue, place a wire rack over a large roasting tray and add 1 litre (4 cups) to the tray. Turn on the outer gas burners for indirect cooking.

Place the pork on the grill racks, put the lid on the barbecue and cook for around 2 hours. Maintain the heat at a medium level by adding a handful of coals every hour. Turn the pork from time to time. If the edges start to blacken or darken too much, just rotate the pork or leave the lid ajar to lower the heat.

Bring the marinade to the boil in a saucepan and reduce to a thick glaze. Just prior to removing the pork from the barbecue, brush it with the glaze and then allow to rest for 15 minutes. Thinly slice the pork before serving.

SERVES 6

1.5 kg pork neck, fat left on

1 quantity Char siu marinade (page 178)

CHORIZO ROLL
FROM
BOROUGH MARKET

SERVES 4

8 fresh chorizo picante, halved

1 bunch wild rocket

2 tablespoons sherry vinegar
(Valdespino would be good)

4 ciabatta rolls, or 1 pide
(Turkish bread) loaf, sliced

extra virgin olive oil

4 Fire-roasted peppers (page 52)

salt

freshly ground black pepper

People queue up for ages at London's famous Borough Market to get their hands on one of Brindisa's barbecued chorizo and pepper rolls. The luscious, smoky chorizo picante is served up with sweet grilled peppers and spicy wild rocket. Team that with the awesome wooded flavour and sharpness of the sherry vinegar — the mere thought of it is making my mouth water!

Chorizo is great to cook on the barbecue, whether it's cured and thinly sliced to wrap around fish, or the fresh, spicy-hot chorizo that needs to be cooked before being eaten. There are many varieties of chorizo but they all have one thing in common: they are made from pork, and get their flavour and colour from smoked paprika.

A little bit of Aioli (page 273) is great with these rolls, and now you won't have to travel all the way to Borough Market to taste them!

Prepare your barbecue for direct grilling. Place the chorizo on the grill and cook until nicely charred on one side, then turn over. There is a lot of fat in chorizo, so if the coals flame up, remove the sausages to a cooler part of the barbecue.

Dress the rocket with the vinegar. Toast the ciabatta or Turkish bread on one side and drizzle with olive oil. Top with slices of roasted pepper and halves of chorizo, add some rocket and season with salt and pepper.

Close the buns and get stuck in.

BISTECCA
ALLA FIORENTINA

SERVES 2–3

1–1.5 kg porterhouse steak

coarse sea salt

2 tablespoons best-quality
extra virgin olive oil

1 garlic clove, smashed

2 rosemary sprigs, bruised

freshly ground black pepper

This beef cut is an Italian cultural icon, one of the most famous steaks in the world. You cannot travel to Tuscany and not see it on the menu. It's known to most people around the world as another cut altogether, porterhouse steak, and is composed of the loin and tenderloin of beef attached to the bone. It's similar to the T-bone but with a greater portion of fillet attached.

Traditionally, the meat for bistecca alla fiorentina is obtained from a breed of animal known as the chianina (pronounced 'kee-a-nee-na'). These cattle have been bred for twenty-two centuries in the Val di Chiana region, particularly the areas surrounding Siena and Arezzo, making it one of the oldest breeds in existence. The size of this steak provides more than enough meat for two or three people to share.

As with most Italian cuisine, the quality of the meat and the simplicity of the preparation make this dish stand out.

Ask your butcher to cut a nice thick steak for you, untrimmed and about three fingers thick. Before cooking, allow the steak to come to room temperature so it isn't chilled in the middle. This will allow it to cook more evenly.

Prepare your barbecue for direct grilling, with one area of the grill hotter than the other. Season the steak with salt and place it over the hottest part of the barbecue.

Cook the steak to a good colour on either side for 5–10 minutes, then move to the lower heat to finish cooking. The thickness of the steak and the fact it is still on the bone will mean you will always have parts that are more cooked than others. Towards the bone will be rare and the outer portions will be medium–well-done.

Once you are happy with the degree of cooking, remove the steak to a tray into which you have placed the olive oil, garlic and rosemary. Allow the steak to rest in the tray for 10 minutes, turning it in the infused oil.

Carve the two sections of meat from the bone and slice. To serve, arrange the steak on a serving platter with the bone, season with salt and pepper, and drizzle with the oil and meat juices.

BARBECUED
BUTTER CHICKEN
TIKKA

This recipe really does benefit from being cooked over coals, as would have been traditional. A few pre-soaked woodchips sprinkled over a gas barbecue will give you some smoke flavour, but it's just not quite the same.

I set up a small kettle barbecue when cooking this dish, as my skewers can rest over both sides of the barbecue, suspending the meat over the flames. If using a gas barbecue, try using two house bricks to suspend the skewers, so that the chicken cooks via radiant heat (like a spit), otherwise the marinade will burn directly onto the grill bars and will adversely affect the flavour.

The chicken skewers can be served on their own with rice and a salad, such as the Pickled cucumber, mint and chilli salad (page 85), but whipping up the butter sauce makes for an awesome alfresco curry. Using any leftover chicken in the sauce the next day works well — kinda like barbecue leftovers!

Combine the marinade ingredients in a food processor and blend well. Thoroughly coat the chicken with the mixture and allow to marinate in the fridge for at least 2 hours.

Meanwhile, to make the butter sauce, combine all the ingredients, except the butter, in a food processor and blend well. Melt the butter in a saucepan over medium heat and when it begins to foam, pour in the sauce mixture and simmer, for 30–40 minutes, until reduced by half, keeping an eye on it so it doesn't catch.

Skewer the chicken pieces onto metal skewers and place on a tray. Drizzle with any remaining marinade and cover while heating your barbecue.

If using charcoal, ensure the coals are well lit and evenly spread, then suspend the skewers over the coals. If using a gas barbecue, cook the skewers over a medium heat, suspended between two house bricks. Cook, turning the skewers frequently to ensure even cooking, for at least 15 minutes to ensure the chicken is cooked through.

When the chicken is well cooked and charred at the edges, un-skewer the meat into the sauce. Alternatively, coat the skewered meat with the sauce.

Serve straight away.

SERVES 4–6

500 g chicken thigh fillets, skin removed, cut into 4 cm dice

MARINADE

80 g (⅓ cup) plain yoghurt

3 garlic cloves, crushed

1 tablespoon ginger paste

1 tablespoon garam masala

2 tablespoons Korean fermented chilli paste (gochujang) or chilli powder

2 tablespoons lime juice

salt, to taste

BUTTER SAUCE

400 g can whole peeled tomatoes

1 onion, roughly chopped

1 red capsicum (pepper), seeds removed

2 teaspoons ginger paste

1 teaspoon garlic paste

1 red chilli, optional

250 ml (1 cup) cream

salt, to taste

50 g butter

BARBECUED BEEF IN BETEL LEAVES

250 g minced beef (not lean)

2 tablespoons palm sugar

2 tablespoons fish sauce

24 betel leaves

SPICE PASTE

2 red chillies, roughly chopped

pinch of salt

1 tablespoon chopped fresh galangal

1 tablespoon chopped coriander root

1 kaffir lime leaf, finely chopped

1 garlic clove, chopped

5 red Asian shallots

Serve these with Sweet chilli sauce (page 269), or with Vietnamese rice noodle salad (page 79). If you absolutely can't get hold of betel leaves, you can use vine leaves instead.

Firstly, make the spice paste by pounding the ingredients in a mortar until smooth.

Combine the spice paste with the beef, palm sugar and fish sauce, mixing well. Cover and set aside in the refrigerator for at least 1 hour.

Soak about 10 bamboo skewers for 1 hour in some water.

Prepare your barbecue for direct grilling over a medium heat, or preferably prepare a charcoal fire.

Wash your betel leaves and pat dry with a clean cloth.

Divide the beef mixture among the betel leaves and wrap them up, enclosing the mince completely. Secure with the soaked bamboo skewers – six betel leaves to a skewer – to make them easier to cook.

Place the skewers directly on the barbecue, or on a rack over the charcoal grill.

Cook the skewers slowly. If the heat at medium is too high, turn several times on the barbecue and move to the resting rack to slowly cook, or turn the heat down on your gas barbecue, so as not to burn the betel leaves – a little charring is unavoidable.

Serve straight away.

BARBECUED
SPICED QUAIL

Quails are such sweet little birds to eat, and you can buy them already boned, which removes any fiddliness from their preparation. These quails are another great little grazing number, and also make a sexy starter if served with the Pickled cucumber, mint and chilli salad (page 85).

Again, try to make a set-up where you can suspend the skewered quail over the heat source without them sitting on the grill rack. A small charcoal kettle barbecue or robata grill is great, but if you can get hold of a satay grill, even better!

In a ceramic dish, marinate the quails in the master stock for at least 2 hours, or overnight.

Soak 12 bamboo skewers for 1 hour in some water.

Prepare your barbecue for direct grilling over a medium heat.

Remove the quails from the stock, reserving the liquid.

Pat the quails dry with a clean cloth. Pierce them with the skewers, through the thigh and the breast, keeping the quail to one end of the skewer.

If using charcoal, ensure the coals are well lit and evenly spread, then suspend the skewers over the coals. If using a gas barbecue, suspend the skewers over two house bricks or on the resting rack over the heat source. Cook the quails evenly on both sides for about 10–12 minutes.

Reboil the reserved stock. Keep about half of the stock simmering, add the rock sugar and reduce to a glaze consistancy. Return the rest to the base master stock in your fridge. Use the glaze to brush over your quails and drizzle all over them at the end.

Remove the quail from the skewers to serve.

SERVES 4

6 medium-large boned quails, leg bones in

500 ml (2 cups) Master stock (page 271)

50 g yellow rock sugar (from Chinese grocers)

BENDER'S
DOUBLE
CHEESE BURGER

SERVES 4

2 tablespoons Japanese mayonnaise (Kewpie)

1 tablespoon American mustard

500 g best-quality minced beef

1 cup roughly chopped flat-leaf parsley

salt

freshly ground black pepper

8 thick slices quality cheddar

4 soft crusty burger rolls, split lengthways

¼ iceberg lettuce, shredded

pickled jalapeño chillies (as many as you like!)

ketchup (optional)

I believe the best burgers are cooked over charcoal, but to achieve a similar result, just add a few pre-soaked woodchips to the barbecue for a smoky flavour.

Prepare your barbecue for direct cooking over a medium heat, or preferably prepare a charcoal fire.

Mix the mayonnaise and mustard together and set aside.

In a large bowl, combine the mince with the parsley, and salt and pepper to season. Mix well, then divide into four even portions.

Divide each portion in half and shape into equal-sized patties.

Place one slice of cheese on top of each of the four patties. Top with the remaining four patties, sandwiching the cheese in between. Press together into four large single patties, ensuring the edges are sealed.

Season the patties lightly. Place directly on the barbecue, or on a rack over the charcoal grill. Cook evenly for about 15 minutes, turning the patties often once they have sealed and the meat is well cooked. Place the remaining cheese slices on top and allow to melt.

Toast the buns on the barbecue, cut side down only, then remove.

Spread a good tablespoon of the mayo mixture onto the base buns. Add the shredded lettuce. Top with the patties, chillies and ketchup, if using.

Top with the other bun half and chomp down.

CHINESE LACQUERED PORK BELLY

This is a beautiful recipe that I regularly whip up — I think pork + Chinese flavours + barbecue is a match made in heaven.

You can do the pre-cooking in your oven, if you prefer, and finish the pork on the barbecue.

Place the pork belly pieces in a deep heatproof dish. Pour the Master stock over and refrigerate for at least 4 hours. Prior to cooking, allow the pork to come close to room temperature.

Prepare your barbecue for indirect cooking over a low heat, or preheat your oven to 100°C.

Cover the pork dish with foil and place in the centre of the barbecue, or in the preheated oven. Cook for 1½–2 hours, until very tender.

Once cooked, remove the pork from the stock, reserving the stock.

Reboil the reserved stock. Keep about 250 ml (1 cup) of the stock simmering, and return the rest to the base master stock in your fridge.

Now add the rock sugar to the reserved stock and boil until the sugar has dissolved.

Place the pork pieces on a tray and brush them with the reduced, syrupy stock.

Prepare your barbecue for direct grilling over a medium heat.

Start steaming the bok choy, broccolini and asparagus separately.

Place the pork pieces directly on the barbecue grill bars. Grill on both sides until the pork is a little crisp at the edges and charred, brushing with the remaining stock to glaze, about 3–5 minutes on each side.

Arrange the steamed vegetables on a large platter. Scatter with the ginger and oyster sauce. Arrange the pork slices on top and garnish with chilli and coriander.

Serve straight away.

SERVES 6

1.5 kg pork belly, cut into two-finger-thick slices — you will end up with about 8 slices

1 quantity Master stock (page 271), at room temperature

50 g rock sugar (available from Chinese grocers)

TO SERVE

2 bunches bok choy (pak choy)

1 bunch broccolini

12 asparagus spears

finely sliced fresh ginger

oyster sauce, for drizzling

1 chilli, finely sliced

½ bunch coriander

PULLED
PORK
SLIDER

MAKES AS MANY AS YOU LIKE

1 quantity Best ever crispy roast pork belly (page 169)

2 small soft burger buns or
1 large burger bun per person

1 quantity Baja sauce (page 259)

Sugar loaf cabbage, coriander and mint salad (page 82)

SAUCE

1 onion, chopped

1 cinnamon stick, broken up

1 star anise

1 teaspoon white peppercorns

250 ml (1 cup) water

1 teaspoon salt

1 teaspoon sugar

2 tablespoons ketchup

1 tablespoon Sweet chilli sauce (page 269), or use ready-made

1 teaspoon English mustard

1 teaspoon kecap manis

This recipe uses the shredded meat from the Best ever crispy pork belly recipe (page 169), which is then tossed through a simple sauce made from common kitchen cupboard ingredients.

Serve the crackle in the bun as a texture treat — if you can keep your hands off it!

To make the sauce, boil together the onion, cinnamon, star anise, peppercorns and water until the water has reduced by half. Discard the cinnamon, star anise and peppercorns.

Add the remaining sauce ingredients to the onion water and puree with a stick blender. Simmer for another 5 minutes and remove from the heat.

Prepare your barbecue for direct cooking over a high heat.

To make the sliders, shred or finely chop the pork belly, keeping the crackling separate.

Add the shredded meat to a roasting tin and place on the barbecue. Add the sauce to moisten the meat and heat well.

Transfer the meat to a serving platter. Serve the buns, Baja sauce and salad separately.

Now invite your guests to build their own sliders — bun, salad, Baja sauce, pork!

BALINESE
BARBECUED
DUCK

SERVES 4

1 whole duck, about 1.4 kg

100 ml coconut cream

½ bunch coriander, washed and shaken dry

SPICE PASTE

5 red Asian shallots, roughly chopped

3 large garlic cloves, peeled

3 large red chillies, roughly chopped

100 g roasted peanuts

1 tablespoon coriander seeds

1 teaspoon cumin seeds

2 cloves

2 green cardamom pods

1 cinnamon stick

2 blades of mace, or ½ teaspoon ground nutmeg

½ teaspoon ground turmeric

1 tablespoon chopped fresh galangal

2 teaspoons ground white pepper

1 lemongrass stem, white part only, chopped

1 teaspoon shrimp paste

1 tablespoon tamarind paste

I love to cook this recipe over charcoal, in either a kamado grill or a small kettle barbecue. I find it easier to pre-cook the duck in the oven first (I know it's cheating!), but finishing it over coals gives it the best flavour; for an equally fantastic result, you can finish the duck on the resting rack of a gas barbecue with some pre-soaked woodchips.

The duck is superb with the Sugar loaf cabbage, coriander and mint salad (page 82) and Nam prik pla dressing (page 270).

Preheat the oven to 100°C, or prepare your barbecue for indirect cooking over a low heat.

Trim off the excess fat from around the duck's neck and bottom. Using a large knife, split the duck in two lengthways, through the back and breast.

Puree all the spice paste ingredients in a blender.

Heat a small frying pan and fry the spice paste for a few minutes, until aromatic. Leave to cool.

Mix half the coconut milk into the spice paste until well combined. Thoroughly rub the mixture all over the duck halves.

Place the duck halves on a roasting rack set inside a roasting tin. Add 500 ml (2 cups) water to the tray, then cover with foil and seal well.

You can now either bake the duck in your preheated oven for 1 hour, or place in the centre of your barbecue and cook indirectly with a low heat for 1 hour with the lid closed.

Remove the duck pieces from the roasting tin. Pierce each duck half with a metal skewer, pushing through the thigh and breast, to skewer each whole half.

Turn the heat up on your barbecue to medium–high. Suspend each duck half over the heat source, or place on the resting rack of your barbecue. Cook with the lid open.

Baste the duck often with the remaining coconut spice mixture, until the duck is crispy and golden, up to 30 minutes. Turn the duck often during this process.

Remove the duck to a board and chop up roughly. Serve straight away, with coriander.

KOREAN PORK WRAPS

Some Korean students were gathered around a barbecue in a park in Brisbane, cooking up this awesome-smelling pork, so I got talking to them about what they were cooking. They were using one of those awful electric barbecues you get in public parks, and had covered it with foil — I suppose to make it hygienic, but also to avoid making an awful mess that they'd later have to clean.

Their barbecue recipe was pretty simple, and then they just rolled the pork in wraps with kimchi, along with a few garnishes that I've Westernised a little here…

Combine all the marinade ingredients in a large bowl. Add the sliced pork spare ribs and thoroughly coat with the mixture. Cover and marinate in the refrigerator for about 2 hours.

Remove the pork from the fridge and allow to come to room temperature.

Prepare your barbecue hotplate for cooking over a medium–high heat. (If, like the Korean kids, you don't want to make a big mess on your hotplate, line it with foil before you start cooking!)

Add a little oil to the hotplate. Add your pork slices and cook quickly, no more than 10 minutes, until well done.

Meanwhile, combine the mayonnaise with the chilli paste to make a chilli mayo. Arrange the avocado, kimchi and lettuce on a serving platter, along with the lime wedges and tortillas.

Transfer the cooked pork to the serving platter.

Now just make yourself a wrap, with as much of each garnish as you like. The avocado will help take the heat out of the chilli mayo.

SERVES 4–6

500 g pork belly spare ribs, sliced into thin strips

sunflower oil, for greasing

3 tablespoons Japanese mayonnaise (Kewpie)

1 tablespoon Korean fermented chilli paste (gochujang), or to taste

2 avocados, sliced

1 cup shredded Kimchi (page 81, or use ready-made)

1 butter lettuce

1 lime, cut into wedges

6 flour tortillas

MARINADE

2 tablespoons sugar

100 ml light soy sauce

4 garlic cloves, finely chopped

100 ml mirin

1 tablespoon toasted sesame oil

1 tablespoon sesame seeds

5 spring onion whites, finely chopped

DUKKAH-CRUSTED
LAMB
CUTLETS

These lamb cutlets make a great canapé or finger food at a barbecue, or you can combine them with a delicious potato salad for a more substantial meal. For ease I use ready-made hummus and dukkah, but you can easily make your own.

Prepare your barbecue for direct cooking over a medium heat. You can use either the fat griddle or the chargrill portion of the barbecue.

Just prior to barbecuing, season the cutlets with salt and pepper. Place on the barbecue and cook to your preferred degree. I prefer medium for lamb, for the best texture and tenderness — so about 3–4 minutes each side.

Remove the cutlets to a tray to rest for 3 minutes.

Just prior to serving, smear about 1 teaspoon of the hummus over the face of each cutlet. Top with a little preserved lemon.

Liberally sprinkle with dukkah to give a nice crunch, then finely scatter with the mint for freshness.

Serve straight away.

SERVES 4

16 French-trimmed lamb cutlets

salt

freshly ground black pepper

250 g ready-made hummus

1 preserved lemon, flesh and pulp removed, skin finely diced

4 tablespoons ready-made dukkah

¼ cup chopped mint

LAMB
SPARE RIBS

4 American-cut 'full rack' lamb ribs

pre-soaked woodchips (optional)

125 ml (½ cup) Glaze, from the
Classic barbecued sticky ribs (page 152)

½ cup chopped mint

RUB

1 tablespoon chopped rosemary

zest of 1 lemon

1 tablespoon flaked salt

½ tablespoon freshly cracked black pepper

1 tablespoon soft brown sugar

These are a great alternative to pork ribs — and about half the price! You'll need to talk to your butcher, as you won't get these at the supermarket.

You can prepare the ribs in your oven, and then finish them on the barbecue to reheat and glaze, or give them the long, slow barbecue love they deserve.

Grind all your rub ingredients in a mortar until well combined. Thoroughly rub the mixture over each side of the lamb ribs. Cover with plastic wrap or a clean cloth and allow to marinate for at least 1 hour at room temperature.

Prepare your barbecue for indirect cooking over a low heat (about 100°C if you have a thermometer).

Remove the excess rub from the ribs. Place them on a tray in the centre of the barbecue, between the heat sources.

Cover with the hood of the barbecue. (Alternatively, cook in the oven on a low heat.) Cook for about 1½ hours, spraying with water every 15 minutes or so to keep the ribs moist. If using the pre-soaked woodchips, periodically add some of them to the barbecue, over the heat source, so they smoulder and smoke.

Once the meat is tender and the bones pull apart with ease, remove the ribs from the barbecue.

Now prepare the barbecue for direct cooking over low heat.

Brush the ribs with the glaze, using a basting brush. Return them to the barbecue. Cook, for about 5 minutes, until the ribs are evenly charred and the glaze is caramelised and bubbling, brushing with more glaze as required.

Remove the ribs to a serving plate. Scatter with the mint for freshness and serve straight away.

LEMONGRASS CHICKEN WINGS

These are just about the best barbecue snack you can get — a large bowl of these will get demolished in no time! This is my interpretation of a recipe by a friend we met at Rainbow Beach, Queensland.

Cut the tips off the chicken wings, then cut each wing into two pieces between the elbow.

Place all the marinade ingredients, except the fish sauce, in a food processor. Blend to a fine paste.

Remove the marinade to a large bowl and taste. Add fish sauce until you get a balanced saltiness.

Add the trimmed chicken wings and coat with the marinade. Cover and refrigerate overnight for maximum flavour penetration.

Prepare your barbecue for cooking over a low to medium heat.

Line the hotplate with baking paper or foil, then lay your chicken wings out. It's best to cook them slowly, for about 15–20 minutes, so they caramelise slowly and cook evenly — there's nothing worse than black yet undercooked chicken wings!

Once well cooked, transfer the wings to a platter and dig in.

SERVES 6–8

2 kg chicken wings

MARINADE

2–3 lemongrass stems, white part only

6 coriander roots, washed

5 red Asian shallots

3 cm piece fresh ginger, peeled

3 garlic cloves

1 teaspoon ground turmeric

1 teaspoon ground white pepper

1 teaspoon Chinese five-spice

1 teaspoon ground cinnamon

2 tablespoons sugar

1 tablespoon tamarind paste

fish sauce, to taste

BULGOGI:
KOREAN
BARBECUED BEEF

SERVES 6

500 g rump or sirloin steak, sliced

3 tablespoons brown sugar or palm sugar

125 ml (½ cup) light soy sauce

4 garlic cloves, finely chopped

good pinch of salt

100 ml rice wine or mirin

2 tablespoons sesame oil

1 tablespoon toasted sesame seeds

1 bunch spring onions, finely sliced

sunflower oil

1 carrot, finely sliced

½ iceberg lettuce, washed
and separated into leaves

1 butterleaf or lollo rosso lettuce

60 ml (¼ cup) Ssamjang (page 268)

200 g Kimchi (page 81)

1 cup mint

Bulgogi is one of Korea's most popular barbecued beef dishes. The word means 'fire meat', and it's often served as an introduction to Korean food for those who are unfamiliar with this style of cooking.

Bulgogi is served with various condiments and wrapped in salad leaves, quite similar to the Chinese san choy bow. As in many Asian cuisines, there is a sense of balance and harmony in a bulgogi, with the flavours of the healthy kimchi, spicy ssamjang and fresh lettuce and herbs.

To make the bulgogi, combine the beef with the sugar, soy sauce, garlic, salt, rice wine, sesame oil, sesame seeds and spring onions. Mix thoroughly and leave to marinate in the refrigerator for a minimum of 2 hours.

Remove the bulgogi from the refrigerator and allow it to come to room temperature.

Heat your barbecue hotplate to medium–hot. Add a little sunflower oil to the hotplate and quickly fry the marinated meat. Add the carrot and cook the beef to desired tenderness — I like to cook to medium.

Transfer the bulgogi to a serving dish.

To serve, take a lettuce leaf and add a little ssamjang, kimchi and bulgogi, top with mint and roll up to make a wrap.

GRILLED
RABBIT
TRAPANI-STYLE

When I visited Sicily once, I ate an amazing meal at a small trattoria in the port city of Trapani, on the western tip of the island. I can't remember the name of the place, but the two things I do remember were the fantastic antipasti trolley and the huge grill in the kitchen, on which all sorts of wonderful fish and meats were being cooked. Several of our party had baby rabbit, which I must admit was probably the most mouth-wateringly tasty rabbit I have ever eaten.

On my return to London I ordered the smallest rabbits I could find and put the dish on the menu at the River Café. I love to serve this dish with Refried beans (page 51).

When buying your rabbits, ask your butcher to split each one down the length of its spine into two halves. Don't trim any belly fat, as this will become lovely and crisp on the barbecue.

Prepare your barbecue for direct grilling over a medium heat.

Dry-rub your rabbits with the dried oregano, followed by the chilli, and then with salt and pepper.

Place the rabbits on the grill, bone side first. Cook for 10 minutes, then turn them over to the skin side and cook for a further 8 minutes, until nicely charred and coloured.

Once cooked, remove to a chopping board. Using a big chopping knife, cut each side into three parts: leg, rib section and shoulder. Place on a serving dish with 1 lemon, cut into wedges.

In a mortar, pound the fresh oregano with a teaspoon of salt to form a fine green paste. Add the juice of the remaining lemon and mix, then add olive oil to make a dressing.

Serve the oregano dressing with the rabbit.

SERVES 6

3 small rabbits, or 2 larger rabbits (each under 1 kg), split down the spine into two halves (ask your butcher to do this)

2 tablespoons dried wild oregano

1 teaspoon chilli flakes

salt

freshly ground black pepper

2 lemons

½ cup fresh oregano

1 teaspoon salt

160 ml extra virgin olive oil

LEMONGRASS AND TURMERIC
PORK RIB
CUTLETS

SERVES 4

500 g fore rib loin cutlets, thinly beaten out

MARINADE

5 red Asian shallots, finely sliced

3 garlic cloves, peeled

3 fat lemongrass stems, white part only, roughly chopped

pinch of salt

1 teaspoon ground white pepper

2 teaspoons ground turmeric

fish sauce, to taste

2 tablespoons sugar

This is one of my 'go to' dishes at any Vietnamese restaurant. It pairs really well with the Vietnamese rice noodle salad (page 79), and is equally delicious with the Pineapple, cucumber and chilli salad (page 76).

Make the marinade by pounding the shallots, garlic, lemongrass and salt in a mortar or food processor until pureed.

Add the pepper, turmeric, fish sauce and sugar.

Thoroughly rub the marinade into the cutlets. Cover and marinate in the refrigerator overnight if possible, or for at least 2 hours.

Prepare your barbecue for direct grilling on a medium–high heat.

Place your beaten-out cutlets directly onto the grill bar over the flames. Cook for 4–5 minutes on each side, until the meat is well done and nicely charred.

Remove from the heat and leave to rest for about 3–4 minutes. Serve straight away.

SPICED SMOKED CHICKEN

I love this recipe. It's a fantastic way to spice up barbecued chicken and use up an abundance of herbs.

Smash the garlic in a mortar with a little salt. Add all the lemon zest and half the lemon juice. Add the curry powder, chilli and olive oil. Season with pepper and mix well.

Remove the excess fat from around the chicken's backside and neck.

Starting at the neck end, carefully separate the skin from the meat, by sliding your hand under the skin, being careful not to break the skin. Do this to the whole chicken.

Using your hands, gently massage the spice paste everywhere under the skin of the chicken, and over the outside.

Prepare your barbecue for indirect cooking over a medium–high heat (180–200°C degrees if you have a thermometer).

Place the chicken directly on the grill, breast side up. Cover with the hood and cook for about 15 minutes, until the chicken begins to colour.

Plunge the herbs into fresh water to wet them well. Lift up the chicken and place the wet herbs directly underneath. Place the chicken over the herbs, bum side up.

Drizzle the remaining lemon juice over the chicken. Replace the hood and cook for 40–45 minutes, until the juices from the chicken run clear when the thigh is pierced.

Once cooked, allow to rest for 10–15 minutes.

SERVES 4

2 garlic cloves, roughly chopped

salt

zest and juice of 2 lemons

2 tablespoons good-quality curry powder

1 dried bird's eye chilli, seeded and crushed

70 ml olive oil

freshly ground black pepper

1 × 1.6 kg chicken

2 bunches rosemary

1–2 bunches fresh bay leaves

1 bunch thyme

GAI YANG: THAI BARBECUED CHICKEN

1.5 kg chicken, cut into 8 joints, trimmed of fat and excess skin

60 ml (¼ cup) coconut cream (skim the top off a cold can of coconut milk)

MARINADE

5 coriander roots, washed and chopped

6 garlic cloves, peeled

5 red Asian shallots, peeled

1 bird's eye chilli

1 tablespoon ground turmeric, or finely chopped fresh turmeric

2 tablespoons ground white pepper

3–4 tablespoons fish sauce, to taste

2–3 tablespoons palm sugar, to taste

My wife spent some time travelling through northern Thailand and Laos, and she still raves about the street food she ate. I asked her if there were any barbecue recipes that stood out from her travels, and without any hesitation she nominated Thai barbecued chicken.

We both love Thai food, so this recipe often makes an appearance at home, served with steamed sticky rice and Som tam: green papaya salad (page 86) plus Sweet chilli sauce (page 269) for extra spice!

For the marinade, use a heavy mortar and pestle or food processor, and puree the coriander roots, garlic, shallots, chilli and turmeric. Add the pepper, fish sauce and sugar to taste, and mix well.

Rub the marinade into and under the skin of the chicken and leave to marinate in the refrigerator for 2–3 hours.

Remove the chicken from the refrigerator and allow it to come to room temperature.

Prepare your barbecue for direct grilling over a medium heat. Just prior to grilling the chicken, add some pre-soaked woodchips. Once they start to smoke, add the chicken. If using gas, heat the woodchips in a smoke box prior to adding the chicken with the gas on high; when the woodchips start to smoke, turn the heat down and start to cook the chicken.

Cook the chicken for 20 minutes or until cooked through. Combine the left-over marinade with the coconut cream and use this to baste the chicken while you cook, turning the pieces frequently to prevent the sugar burning.

VIETNAMESE GRILLED BEEF

These fragrant beef strips are delicious tossed through Vietnamese rice noodle salad (page 79) for a traditional bun bo salad.

Make the marinade by pounding the shallots, garlic, lemongrass and salt in a mortar or food processor until pureed. Add the pepper, turmeric and fish sauce.

Rub the marinade into the steak and leave to marinate in the refrigerator — overnight if possible, or for at least 2 hours.

Prepare your barbecue for direct grilling over a high heat. Cook the beef to medium at the most, about 3–4 minutes each side depending on the thickness of the steak.

Leave the steak to rest, then slice thinly.

Serve straight away with the Vietnamese rice noodle salad (page 79).

SERVES 6

500–600 g rump steak

MARINADE

5 red Asian shallots, finely sliced

3 garlic cloves, peeled

2 fat lemongrass stems, white part only, finely chopped

pinch of salt

1 teaspoon ground white pepper

3 teaspoons ground turmeric

fish sauce, to taste

TIKKA
LAMB
CUTLETS

SERVES 4–6

16 lamb cutlets

vegetable oil, for greasing

2 onions, sliced

lemon wedges

MARINADE

3 tablespoons plain yoghurt

2 garlic cloves, crushed

1 tablespoon ginger paste

1 tablespoon garam masala

1 tablespoon Korean fermented chilli paste
(gochujang) or chilli powder

2 tablespoons lime juice

salt, to taste

This was the first Indian–style meat dish my son Herb ate at a particular restaurant in Whitechapel in London. Strange that he devoured these cutlets at the age of three, but by the time he was eight he wouldn't go near them.

Serve these cutlets with either Spiced red bean salad (page 88), Whole pumpkin biryani (page 58) or Sugar loaf cabbage, coriander and mint salad (page 82).

Combine all the marinade ingredients in a food processor and blend well. Thoroughly coat the lamb with the mixture and allow to marinate in the fridge for at least 2 hours.

Prepare your barbecue for direct cooking on a medium to high heat. Lightly oil the grill plate of your barbecue.

Remove the excess marinade from the lamb. Lay the cutlets out evenly on the grill plate. Cook the lamb to medium-rare, about 3–4 minutes on each side.

Remove the cutlets to a serving platter to rest.

Before scraping the barbecue plate, quickly fry the onions on the same area the cutlets were cooked on, so they pick up the flavours of the marinade and soften slightly, but still have a crunchy texture.

Serve the cutlets and onions straight away, with lemon wedges.

SMOKED BEEF SHORT RIBS
WITH NAM PRIK PLA

Prepare your barbecue for indirect cooking over a low heat.

Puree all the spice puree ingredients in a blender. Rub the spice puree all over the beef ribs and place in a deep baking tray. Pour in the stock and tightly cover with foil.

Place the tray on the barbecue, between the heat sources. Close the hood on your barbecue and cook for 2 hours, until the ribs are tender. If your barbecue does not have a hood, you can cook the ribs on a low heat in the oven and finish them on your barbecue just prior to serving.

Meanwhile, soak the woodchips for 1 hour in some water.

Once the ribs are cooked, remove them from the baking tray, reserving the cooking liquid. Place the ribs on the resting rack.

Turn up the heat of the barbecue by igniting the centre burners. Combine the sweet chilli sauce with some of the reserved cooking liquid, then use some of it to glaze the ribs.

Add half the pre-soaked woodchips to the grill plate so they start to smoke. Close the hood of the barbecue. Smoke and roast the ribs so they caramelise – this will take around 10 minutes.

Glaze the ribs again and add the remaining woodchips to the grill plate. Close the hood again. When nicely smoked and glazed, about 10 minutes, remove the ribs to a serving dish.

Shred the meat off the bones. Serve with the nam prik pla sauce.

SERVES 4–6

6 beef short ribs

500 ml (2 cups) chicken stock

2 cups woodchips

60 ml (¼ cup) Sweet chilli sauce (page 269)

1 quantity Nam prik pla (page 270)

SPICE PUREE

2 garlic cloves

5 red Asian shallots

2 tablespoons palm sugar

1 lemongrass stem, white part only, chopped

1 long dried chilli

100 ml fish sauce

SWEETS
and
DRINKS

GRILLED PINEAPPLE WITH RUM, GINGER
AND LEMONGRASS SYRUP

BAKED PEARS AND APPLES

BANOFFEE PIE, MY WAY

BARBECUED PEACHES

BARBECUED BANANA SPLIT

HOTCAKES

SWEET BRUSCHETTA

LIME AND HONEY POSSET

MIXED-BERRY MERINGUE SWISS ROLL

KNICKERBOCKER GLORY

CREMINO

**DAMPER DOUGHNUTS WITH
MARSHMALLOWS**

SUMMER PUDDING

BANANA TARTIN

LEMON CURD CUPS

VANILLA CHEESECAKE WITH BERRIES

MARSHMALLOWS

CAIPIRINHA

MOJITO

LEMONADE

RUSTIE'S CARIBBEAN COOLER

GINGER BEER

LIMEADE

PIMM'S

SOUTHERN CROSS PIMM'S

DARK AND STORMY

MARGARITA

GRILLED
PINEAPPLE
WITH
RUM, GINGER AND
LEMONGRASS SYRUP

SERVES 4

1 pineapple, skin removed, flesh cut into quarters lengthways

SYRUP

200 ml water

100 ml white rum

100 g sugar

3 cm piece fresh ginger, sliced

1 lemongrass stem, bruised

zest and juice of 1 lemon

zest and juice of 1 lime

1 dried red chilli

SPICED SUGAR

1 dried red chilli

2 teaspoons crystal salt

3 teaspoons caster sugar

Ben, my pastry chef from the Atlantic Bar and Grill in London, met a Thai girl and travelled to Thailand to meet her family. He came back from his travels inspired by the wonderful food he'd experienced, and was particularly enthused by this recipe for grilled fruit.

The really exciting thing about this recipe is the sugar and salt condiment that's served with the fruit. I've come across this spiced sugar before, in David Thompson's kitchen at Nahm in London. The sweet–salty flavours created are so typically Thai. The recipe here is just a guide, as these things are best done according to personal taste. If you prefer more chilli, then add it. With the salt and sugar it's about finding the balance that's right for you, but I would recommend that you err on the side of sweet!

To make the syrup, place all the ingredients in a saucepan and bring to the boil, making sure the sugar has dissolved. Remove from the heat and cool, then strain.

Marinate the pineapple in the syrup overnight.

To make the spiced sugar, pound the dried chilli and salt in a mortar until you have fine flakes of chilli. Add the caster sugar.

Prepare your barbecue for cooking on a medium–high heat. Place the pineapple over the heat and barbecue until caramelised, turning the fruit as required.

Once cooked, skewer the pineapple with bamboo sticks and serve with the spiced sugar as a dipping condiment.

BAKED
PEARS
AND
APPLES

The humble pear and apple are often overlooked when it comes to barbecues. In the UK they are more likely to turn up in the form of perry (pear cider) or apple cider at your average backyard get-together — not that there's anything wrong with that!

Pears or apples stuffed with a lovely mix of dried fruit, nuts and booze are a real treat. They're wrapped in foil then thrown on the coals to cook while you're preparing the meat or other dishes. When you're ready to serve, accompany them with lashings of cream or ice cream.

Soak the raisins in the booze overnight, or simmer together in a saucepan for 5 minutes and then allow to cool. Drain, reserving the liquid.

With a small knife, cut around the apples or pears horizontally, about 1 cm deep.

Combine the butter, raisins, sugar, nuts and spices, and stuff into the hollowed-out cores of the fruit.

Prepare your barbecue for cooking on a medium–high heat.

Wrap each fruit completely in foil twice and place next to the coals or above the heat source and cook for 40 minutes.

Serve while hot, drizzled with the reserved, reduced raisin liquid.

MAKES 4

2 tablespoons raisins (or other dried fruit, such as chopped dates)

100 ml brandy or rum

4 pears or apples (or a mixture of both), cored

100 g butter, softened

2 tablespoons soft brown sugar

2 tablespoons flaked almonds (or other nuts, such as pecans)

2–3 grates of whole nutmeg, to taste

¼ teaspoon ground cinnamon

BANOFFEE PIE MY WAY

**MAKES
8 PIES**

PASTRY

350 g butter, cold

500 g plain flour

150 g icing sugar

3 egg yolks

rice, for blind-baking

FILLING

395 g can condensed milk

100 g good-quality dark chocolate
(70% cocoa)

200 g crème fraîche

250 g mascarpone

4 large bananas, sliced

CHOCOLATE SAUCE

100 ml cream

100 g good-quality dark chocolate
(70% cocoa)

Banoffee pie is a true modern classic of English home cooking. It was invented some time in the 1970s, apparently in East Sussex, and its popularity in England is amazing. Therefore, it cannot be left out of an English barbecue experience.

The name comes from the pie's combination of banana and toffee, which is created by cooking a can of condensed milk. My variation on the classic uses the caramelised condensed milk to create a ripple effect, and the pie is finished with a drizzle of chocolate sauce. James Martin gave me the idea for this twist.

Prepare the pastry by rubbing the butter into the flour and sugar until a fine crumb is achieved. Add the egg yolks and bring together until combined. Wrap in plastic wrap and chill for at least 2 hours.

Place the unopened can of condensed milk in a heavy-bottomed saucepan, cover with water and simmer for 3 hours. Keep covered with water at all times, as otherwise the can could explode! Remove after 3 hours and allow to cool completely.

Roll out the pastry and line individual tartlet tins, leaving the pastry hanging over the sides. Cover the pastry with baking paper. Fill with rice and blind-bake for 20 minutes, until the pastry is set but not coloured. Remove the rice and continue to bake for 10 minutes, until the pastry is golden and crisp.

Allow to cool, then trim the edges of the pastry.

To make the filling, melt the chocolate and line the inside of each tartlet tin with a thin layer of melted chocolate.

Combine the crème fraîche and mascarpone in a bowl, then fold through the caramelised condensed milk to create a ripple effect.

Spoon the caramel into the tarts and top with slices of banana.

To make the chocolate sauce, heat the cream until just boiling. Remove from the heat, add the chocolate and mix until completely melted.

Drizzle the sauce over the pies and serve straight away.

BARBECUED
PEACHES

Peaches are just about the perfect summer fruit. Grilled and accompanied by a smooth dollop of something simple like crème fraîche, they make the perfect finale to any barbecue, and they're so easy to prepare. Leave the peaches to rest for a little after they've been grilled, so their juices slowly ooze to make a wonderful syrup. Other summer fruit work equally well — try apricots, nectarines or even mangoes. The natural sugars will caramelise and you'll get a great sweet, smoky flavour coming through.

Prepare your barbecue for cooking on a medium–high heat.

Place the peaches on the grill, flesh side down. Cook for 5 minutes, then turn the peaches 90 degrees so you get a crisscross pattern from the grill.

Turn the peaches over gently, sprinkle with brandy and a little vanilla sugar, and cook for a further 2–3 minutes.

Serve each with a good dollop of crème fraîche, garnished with mint.

SERVES 6

6 ripe peaches (they must be ripe), halved and stoned

6 teaspoons brandy

2 tablespoons vanilla sugar

250 g crème fraîche

1 tablespoon chopped mint

BARBECUED
BANANA
SPLIT

6 ripe bananas, unpeeled

1 Snickers bar, thinly sliced

1–2 tablespoons runny honey

1–2 tablespoons crushed salted peanuts

cream or ice cream
(vanilla — or honeycomb if you're game),
to serve

Caroline, a good friend of mine, gave me this cracking barbecue recipe. It's nothing revolutionary, but it really appealed to me because I love the combination of bananas and peanut butter.

You need a sweet tooth for this one, so don't say I didn't warn you! Be prepared for the kids to start bouncing off the walls. This is a great recipe to make when you're going camping or having a barbecue in the great outdoors as you can prepare the bananas in advance and they travel well.

Prepare your barbecue for cooking on a medium heat.

Use a sharp knife to make an incision along the length of each banana, being careful not to cut all the way through.

Insert slices of the Snickers bar into the slit bananas, dividing the chocolate equally between the fruit. Drizzle with a little honey, sandwich the bananas back together and wrap in foil.

Place over the direct heat of the barbecue and cook for 5 minutes on each side.

When cooked, unwrap the bananas, sprinkle with the crushed peanuts and serve with cream or ice cream.

HOTCAKES

These are great for breakfast, or you could serve them later in the day cooked on the barbecue. The combined flavour of bananas and dates, pecans and maple syrup is awesome. Serve them with cream or some great-quality vanilla ice cream.

Hotcakes, or griddle cakes, are a classic American speciality, similar to big, thick pikelets. They are most often eaten for breakfast, served with maple syrup or bacon, and are generally cooked on a large skillet or in a griddle pan. This makes them perfect for the barbecue hotplate.

To make the hotcakes, combine the flour, baking powder, sugar, cinnamon and half the chopped nuts. Add the egg and slowly pour in the milk until a thick batter is achieved that will drop but not be too runny. Mix in the dates and allow to rest.

Prepare your barbecue for cooking on a medium heat. Melt a little butter on the barbecue hotplate or in a nonstick pan. Half-fill crumpet rings with batter to get nice round shapes with depth. When bubbles and little holes appear on top of the hotcakes, turn them over to finish cooking.

To serve, remove the crumpet rings and top the hotcakes with sliced banana and a scoop of ice cream. Drizzle with maple syrup and scatter with the remaining nuts.

MAKES 8–10

300 g plain flour

1 tablespoon baking powder

1 tablespoon caster sugar

1 teaspoon ground cinnamon

½ cup chopped pecans
(or nuts of your choice)

1 large egg

280 ml milk

½ cup chopped dates
(Medjool dates are best)

butter, for greasing

3 bananas, sliced

ice cream, to serve

maple syrup, to drizzle

SWEET
BRUSCHETTA

These lovely fruity bruschetta remind me
of a homemade fruit Danish. Serve with
some clotted cream, crème fraîche or ice
cream. They can be served as a dessert or
as a fun breakfast or brunch — the choice
is yours. It's also a great way to use up
slightly overripe fruit.

SERVES 4

4 slices sourdough bread, each 1.5 cm thick

80 g butter, plus an extra 4 small knobs

3 tablespoons soft brown sugar

80 ml (⅓ cup) brandy

1 vanilla bean, split

2 peaches, stoned and quartered

2 nectarines, stoned and quartered

4 apricots, stoned and halved

Prepare your barbecue for indirect cooking on a high heat,
though you'll be toasting the sourdough on a direct heat.

Toast the sourdough slices over the direct heat of the coals
or gas. Butter the toasted bruschetta on both sides and
place on a roasting tray.

Combine sugar, brandy, scraped vanilla bean and seeds.
Toss in all the fruit and allow to macerate for 10 minutes.

Divide the fruit evenly between the toasted bruschetta and
drizzle with the juices. Top with the knobs of butter.

Place the tray between the heat sources for indirect cooking,
close the lid and cook for 15 minutes.

When cooked, the fruit should be soft and lightly caramelised,
and the edges of the bruschetta crispy. Serve straight away.

LIME
AND
HONEY
POSSET

A posset is a very simple, set cooked cream —
an English version of panna cotta.

Possets are so easy to make and they taste
sensational. They're great served with fresh
fruit to counter the sweet creaminess. A classic
posset is made with lemon juice, as you need
the acidity to set the cream. You can also use
lime, as in this recipe, or a combination of
lemon, lime and orange.

SERVES 6

750 ml (3 cups) thickened (whipping) cream

zest and juice of 3 limes, or 1 lemon

175 g honey

1 mango, finely diced

6 mint sprigs

Heat the cream in a saucepan to 75°C. Remove from
the heat and cool slightly to 65°C.

Add the lime zest, juice and honey to the cream and
mix well to dissolve the honey; you should notice that
the mixture thickens slightly.

Allow to cool, then pour into six cups or glasses.
Place the possets on a tray, cover each with plastic wrap
and leave to set in the refrigerator for about 4 hours.

Serve topped with the mango and garnished with a mint sprig.

MIXED-BERRY
MERINGUE
SWISS ROLL

This recipe is very simple to prepare. The crunch of the meringue and almonds, combined with the sweet sharpness of the berries, makes it an English pavlova! I first saw a fantastic cook called Mary Berry prepare the basic recipe for this dessert on a UK cooking show called *Daily Cooks*, and I've used it many times since.

I would recommend a gas barbecue for this one, and it also works well in a conventional oven.

Prepare your barbecue for indirect cooking over a high heat (200°C if you have a thermometer).

Whisk the egg whites with ¼ cup of the caster sugar until just stiff. Add the remaining sugar and whisk until the mixture is stiff and glossy.

Grease a baking tray with butter and line with baking paper. Spoon the meringue over the paper evenly, then sprinkle with flaked almonds.

Place the tray between the heat sources for indirect cooking and close the lid. Cook at 200°C for 8–10 minutes, or until the almonds are golden. Keep an eye on things at this stage.

Open the barbecue and cool slightly. Close the lid, reduce the heat to around 160°C and cook for a further 15–20 minutes, or until firm to the touch.

Spread out a piece of baking paper, around the same size as the meringue, and dust with icing sugar. When the meringue is ready, turn it out onto the paper. Remove the baking paper from the bottom and allow to cool.

To make the filling, whip the cream with the scraped seeds from the vanilla bean. Spread the cream evenly over the meringue, then scatter the mixed berries over the cream.

Starting from the long edge of the meringue, roll up tightly, using the paper to help lift and roll. Secure the roll tightly, leaving it wrapped in the paper, and chill for 45 minutes inthe refrigerator.

Serve the meringue roll garnished with mint leaves, and accompanied by additional fresh berries.

SERVES 8

4 large egg whites
1 cup caster sugar
butter, for greasing
50 g flaked almonds
icing sugar, for dusting
mint leaves, to garnish
extra berries, to serve

FILLING

300 ml thickened (whipping) cream
1 vanilla bean, split
50 g raspberries
50 g blackberries
50 g blueberries
100 g strawberries, quartered

KNICKERBOCKER
GLORY

SERVES 4

300 ml whipping cream

100 g dark chocolate (70% cocoa),
roughly chopped

250 g strawberries, hulled and quartered

50 g icing sugar

8 scoops vanilla ice cream

200 g ready-made chocolate brownies,
crumbled

50 g ready-made peanut brittle bar,
roughly chopped

1 cup dried sliced coconut, toasted

4 mint sprigs

Firstly, make your sauces. Pour 100 ml of the cream into a small saucepan and heat until almost boiling. Add the chocolate, whisk until smooth and set aside.

For the strawberry sauce, combine the strawberries and icing sugar in a small saucepan. Bring to the boil. Transfer to a blender and puree until smooth. Set aside.

Whip the remaining cream.

Divide all the crumbled brownies among four chilled glasses. Place one scoop of ice cream in each glass.

Top with half the chocolate sauce and half the strawberry sauce.

Add some peanut brittle and whipped cream.

Repeat in the same order, finishing with the whipped cream.

Garnish with the coconut and mint. Serve straight away.

CREMINO

To make the meringue, combine the sugar and 1 cup water in a small saucepan. Simmer over medium heat, stirring until the sugar has dissolved.

Cook the sugar syrup for 10–15 minutes, until it reaches the 'soft ball' stage — about 115°C on a thermometer. If you don't have a sugar thermometer, dip a spoon into the syrup and then into ice water – the syrup should be able to be moulded with your fingers into a soft ball.

In a clean, grease-free bowl, start whisking the egg whites with the cream of tartar, using an electric mixer, until soft peaks form.

Bring the sugar syrup to the 'hard ball' stage — about 121°C on a thermometer.

Increase the electric mixer speed to high. With the motor running, gradually pour the sugar syrup into the beaten egg whites. Now beat at medium speed for 15–20 minutes, or until the meringue has cooled to room temperature and is thick and glossy.

Transfer the meringue to a piping bag. Set aside until required.

To make the chocolate filling, warm the milk in a saucepan over low heat.

In a separate saucepan, mix the flour, sugar and scraped vanilla seeds until smooth. Whisk in the warm milk, a little at a time, until smooth.

Cook over a gentle heat for 10 minutes, stirring continuously until thick.

Remove the pan from the heat and stir in the chocolate, Nutella and butter.

Divide the chocolate mixture among cappuccino cups, glasses or small bowls. Allow to cool, cover with plastic wrap and place in the refrigerator to set.

Just prior to serving, spoon some gelato or ice cream into each cup. Crumble the biscuits over the top. Pipe the meringue around and over the top of each cup.

Using a kitchen blow torch, toast the top of the meringues.

Serve straight away.

MAKES 8

8 scoops salted caramel gelato or chocolate peanut butter ice cream (1 scoop per person)

8 amaretti biscuits

ITALIAN MERINGUE

1 cup caster sugar

4 egg whites

pinch of cream of tartar

CHOCOLATE FILLING

500 ml milk

2 tablespoons plain flour

2 tablespoons caster sugar

1 vanilla bean, split

100 g dark chocolate

100 g hazelnut chocolate spread, such as Nutella

50 g unsalted butter

DAMPER
DOUGHNUTS
WITH
MARSHMALLOWS

SERVES 12

1 quantity Damper dough (page 14)

12 Marshmallows (page 247)

SYRUP

½ cup shaved palm sugar or light brown sugar

zest and juice of 2 limes

125 ml (½ cup) dark rum
(Bundaberg would be good)

500 ml (2 cups) vegetable oil or sunflower oil

This recipe was inspired by the television series *The Great BBQ Challenge*, in which aspiring grill masters were pitted against each other to vie for the title of Australian BBQ Champion.

During one of the challenges, the contestants had to make a fire-cooked meal for a team of army training personnel. One of the recipes they came up with was doughnuts made from Damper, that great Aussie bush-cooking invention. With a little instruction from yours truly, their damper doughnuts turned out amazingly well.

These doughnuts are best served warm, with vanilla ice cream.

To make the doughnuts, form the damper dough into small balls, about the size of golf balls. Pat each ball out flat and place a marshmallow in the centre. Fold the dough over and crimp the edges to seal the marshmallow inside. Allow to rest.

To make the syrup, place the sugar, lime zest, juice and rum in a saucepan and bring to the boil. Reduce until you have a thin syrup, then set aside.

Heat the oil in a wok over a medium heat, or on the side burner of your barbecue, until it reaches 170°C. You can test if it's hot enough by dropping a small amount of dough into the oil — it should brown in about 10 seconds.

Carefully place a few doughnuts at a time into the hot oil, and cook until golden and puffy. Allow to drain for a few minutes on paper towel, then place in the syrup so they soak it up.

Serve the doughnuts straight away while they're warm.

SUMMER
PUDDING

If there's one thing the English do well it's puddings. And summer pudding has to be right at the top of the list. Using plain old white bread, plus loads of fresh or frozen berries, some nice red wine and sugar, it's thrifty!

I could not imagine a better end to a sensational summer barbecue than the sharp, sweet flavours of a summer pudding. It's best prepared a day in advance, which is nice because you can whip it out at the end of the meal with little fuss.

Accompany the pudding with some Greek-style yoghurt or crème fraîche.

Sprinkle the sugar into a heavy-based saucepan. Pour the water over and stir to make a paste. Cook to a light golden caramel.

Add the scraped vanilla bean and seeds, black pepper and wine, and bring to the boil. Simmer for 10 minutes, until reduced by half. Remove from the heat and gently stir in the fruit. Leave to stand until cold, then add the basil.

Line a glass bowl evenly with the bread slices, overlapping them so there are no gaps.

Fill the lined bowl with your cooled berry compote, then cover the top with overlapping slices of bread. Cover with plastic wrap and place a plate on top to weigh the pudding down; the plate should be the same diameter as the pudding, but slightly smaller than the bowl. Refrigerate overnight.

When ready to serve, turn the pudding out onto a large serving plate, or serve it straight from the bowl.

SERVES 6

150 g caster sugar

50 ml water

1 vanilla bean, split

1–2 teaspoons freshly ground black pepper, to taste

500 ml (2 cups) fruity light red wine (grenache or valpolicella are good)

600 g mixed summer fruit (strawberries, raspberries, blueberries, blackberries, etc.)

1 tablespoon chopped basil

1 loaf sliced white bread, crusts removed

BANANA
TARTIN

SERVES 4

2 sheets ready-rolled frozen puff pastry, thawed (2 bases per sheet)

200 g soft brown sugar or palm sugar

50 g unsalted butter

1 teaspoon vanilla extract

4 large bananas, ripe but not too soft

good pinch of salt

4 blini pans or silicon tart moulds

ice cream, to serve

This is a bad-ass way to end a meal on the barbecue!

Blini pans are small frying pans about 8cm in diameter and silicon tart moulds are flexible moulds used in baking. Both are available from good cooking stores and are great things to have in the kitchen.

Cut the pastry into rounds 2 cm wider than your moulds, so that you can tuck the edges into each mould. Cover the pastry and set aside in the fridge until required.

Place the sugar in a small saucepan and add a few tablespoons water. Place over medium heat and bring to the boil. Gently swirl the sugar and water to help the dissolve the sugar.

When the sugar begins to caramelise and you see darkish brown spots, remove the pan from the heat. Whisk in the butter and vanilla extract.

Divide the caramel among the four pans or moulds.

Peel the bananas and trim off the ends so the bananas are square.

Cut the bananas into 3 cm lengths; you should end up with 4–5 pieces per mould. Arrange these in the centre of each pan or mould.

Cover with the pastry rounds, pushing the edges down around the bananas. (These can now be set aside to be cooked later.)

Prepare your barbecue for indirect cooking over a medium heat (with the outer heat elements on, and the inside one off).

Place the pans or moulds directly on a baking tray, then into the middle of your barbecue. Bake for 15–20 minutes with the hood closed, until the pastry is golden and puffed up.

Once baked, allow to rest for a minute, then turn out onto individual plates.

Season to taste and serve straight away, with your favourite ice cream on top.

LEMON CURD CUPS

These are a yummy twist on a lemon meringue pie, perfect for a summer barbecue dessert. Keep some extra liqueur in the freezer for a great little tipple!

First, make your lemon curd. Combine the lemon zest, lemon juice, eggs and egg yolks in a saucepan with the butter and sugar.

Whisk over medium heat for about 10 minutes, until thickened — keep whisking continuously so the eggs don't scramble.

Transfer to a bowl to cool.

Divide the cake cubes among six nice serving glasses, cappuccino cups or small bowls.

Pour the liqueur over the cake cubes, then crumble half the meringues over the top.

Layer the lemon curd over the meringue. Add the whipped cream and top with the remaining meringue. Garnish with a sprig of mint.

These will keep in the fridge for a few hours.

SERVES 6

zest and juice of 4 lemons

4 eggs, plus 4 egg yolks

200 g unsalted butter

160 g caster sugar

200 g pound cake or madeira cake, cut into small cubes

120 ml Limoncello or other lemon liqueur

1 box of ready-made meringue pieces

500 ml (2 cups) whipping cream, softly whipped

6 mint sprigs

VANILLA CHEESECAKE WITH BERRIES

80 g butter, softened

100 g biscuit crumbs

1 vanilla bean, split

400 g crème fraîche or sour cream

500 g cream cheese

250 g icing sugar, sifted, plus extra for dusting

4 large eggs

400 g raspberries

Everyone loves a good cheesecake. Served with fresh berries, it's a great pudding to pull out at the end of a barbecue. Use good-quality Anzac or sweet oat biscuits to make the base.

There is only one real cheesecake and that's a cooked one, prepared in the traditional American style. Set cheesecakes just don't have the same flavour and texture. This recipe is based on the method I learnt while cooking for Ruth Rogers at the River Café. I cooked quite a few meals at her home for some pretty amazing people and on one evening we cooked this particular dessert.

You can cook this cheesecake on a gas barbecue, but it's safer to try it in the oven first. It needs to be prepared the day before you want to serve it so that it sets properly.

Preheat the oven to 150°C or prepare your barbecue for indirect cooking. Heavily grease a 25 cm springform cake tin with butter. Throw in the biscuit crumbs and roll the tin around to coat the sides. The excess crumbs should cover the base in an even layer.

In a bowl, stir the seeds from the scraped vanilla bean into the crème fraîche until smooth.

Beat the cream cheese with the icing sugar until soft and smooth. Add the eggs, one at a time, beating well after each addition. Fold in the crème fraîche mixture and mix thoroughly, then pour into the prepared tin. Bang the tin down on the bench to remove any air bubbles.

Transfer the cheesecake to the preheated oven or barbecue and bake on a baking tray on the lowest shelf for 50–60 minutes, until the centre just wobbles and the cake is just golden on top. Don't worry if the top doesn't colour very much; it's more important that the centre is cooked so that it just wobbles, but doesn't crack. Rest the cheesecake for at least 5 hours to cool and become firm.

When ready to serve, turn out the cheesecake. Top with raspberries and a dusting of extra icing sugar, and slice into wedges.

MARSHMALLOWS

Who hasn't been camping and toasted marshmallows over the fire? They are just great. Kids love them, and now you have the recipe you won't need to buy them.

You can experiment with this recipe by adding different combinations of fruit and nuts and dipping the marshmallow in chocolate. You could even make your own rocky road! I love adding roasted hazelnuts or raspberries, and you could also try dried cherries or other dried fruit.

Place the mineral water, glucose and the 450 g icing sugar in a saucepan and bring to the boil.

Soak the gelatine leaves in cold water for 5 minutes or until soft, then squeeze out the excess liquid and dissolve in the syrup.

Whisk the egg whites with the scraped vanilla seeds until they have soft peaks and are white in colour. Start pouring the syrup into the egg whites and continue to whisk until stiff and doubled in volume and the mixture is cool. Whip until cooled to room temperature (around 10–15 minutes).

Combine the cornflour and the additional icing sugar, and dust some of the mixture over a tray covered in baking paper. Fill a piping bag with the egg white mixture and pipe marshmallows the size of ping pong balls onto the tray.

Dust the tops of the marshmallows well with more of the cornflour and icing sugar mixture and let them stand for 4 hours, until completely set. If you let them stand overnight they will go slightly crusty, which is fine.

The marshmallows will keep for a week if stored in an airtight container.

SERVES 6

150 ml still mineral water

50 g liquid glucose

450 g icing sugar, plus an extra 200 g icing sugar

6 gelatine leaves

2 large egg whites

1 vanilla bean, split

200 g cornflour

CAIPIRINHA

I have worked with a lot of Brazilians over the years, and if there's one thing I've discovered it's that they love a barbecue.

This is probably one of the most famous drinks to come out of Brazil, and it tastes sensational! It's made with cachaça, a spirit made from sugar-cane juice, combined with the refreshing flavours of lime and good sugar.

SERVES 1

2 teaspoons soft brown sugar

½ juicy lime

crushed ice

50 ml cachaça

Muddle the sugar and lime in the bottom of a glass tumbler.

Fill the glass with crushed ice and stir.

Pour over the cachaça and stir again.

Remember to sip!

MOJITO

The mojito is a classic Cuban cocktail — long, cool and sexy, and just perfect for a barbecue. The wonderful balance of sweet and sour flavours pairs really well with the smoky, sticky flavour of Classic barbecued sticky ribs (page 152), Char siu duck (page 178) or Char siu pork (page 181).

SERVES 1

1 tablespoon soft brown sugar

½ lime, cut into wedges

8 mint leaves

crushed ice

50 ml Havana Club white rum

15 ml seven-year-old Havana Club dark rum

Muddle the sugar, lime wedges and mint leaves in a highball glass. Fill the glass with crushed ice.

Pour the white rum over the ice and mix thoroughly.

Float the dark rum over the top.

Drink straight away.

LEMONADE

My wife and kids always make jugs of home-made lemonade when we put on a Vietnamese-style barbecue in our backyard. Lemonade is certainly not traditionally associated with Vietnamese food, but it's a refreshing drink and it goes so well with spicy South-East Asian flavours.

SERVES 5

juice of 5 unwaxed lemons

zest of 1 unwaxed lemon

1 cup golden caster sugar or plain caster sugar

ice cubes

thin lemon slices

Combine the lemon juice and zest with the caster sugar until the desired level of sweetness is achieved. Stir until the sugar is dissolved.

Place ice cubes in tall glasses and pour in the lemon and sugar syrup.

Add water to taste, and stir to dilute.

Garnish with lemon slices and serve straight away.

RUSTIE'S
CARIBBEAN
COOLER

I get to work with some fantastic people on TV. One person who is larger than life is Rustie Lee. She came up with this recipe and I thought it would make the perfect barbecue drink. If you want to enjoy it without the white rum, replace the spirit with water.

Rustie is from the Caribbean, so it makes sense that this drink would go well with Jerked chicken (page 164) or even Mexican suckling pig tortillas (page 148). Anything with a bit of spice!

MAKES
1.5 LITRES
(6 CUPS)

250 g ripe or overripe strawberries

zest and juice of 2 limes

100 ml white rum

100 ml maple syrup

1 litre (4 cups) ginger ale

crushed ice

lime slices

quartered strawberries

mint leaves

Place the strawberries, lime zest, lime juice and rum in a blender. Pulse to combine.

Add the maple syrup and ginger ale, and stir.

Pour into glasses over crushed ice. Garnish with lime slices, strawberries and mint leaves.

Serve straight away.

GINGER BEER

Ginger beer is such a refreshing drink.
It's also an essential ingredient in my favourite
cocktail, the Dark and stormy (page 255).

MAKES ABOUT
3 LITRES
(12 CUPS)

3 litres (12 cups) boiled water, cooled to lukewarm

300 g coconut sugar or golden caster sugar

100 ml lime juice

3 tablespoons ginger paste
(best made using young ginger)

2 tablespoons brewer's yeast

ice cubes

lime slices

mint leaves

Combine the lukewarm boiled water, sugar, lime juice,
ginger paste and yeast in a stainless steel pot. Stir well.
Cover with a lid and leave to brew overnight.

The next day, skim off any impurities that have risen
to the surface.

Transfer to two clean 1.5 litre soft drink bottles, using
a funnel and a sieve. Don't fill the bottles to the top!

Secure the lids and place in the fridge. Keep as cold as possible,
to inhibit the action of the yeast.

To serve, fill a jug with ice cubes and lime slices.
Slap some mint leaves in your hands to bruise them and
release their fragrance, then add to the jug. Top with the
ginger beer and serve.

LIMEADE

To spice it up, add your favourite white spirit
or rum!

MAKES ABOUT
1.5 LITRES

juice of 10 fat limes

1 cup coconut sugar or golden caster sugar

2 kaffir lime leaves, finely sliced

1 lemongrass stem, smashed

ice cubes

soda water

Combine the lime juice and sugar in a jug.
Stir to dissolve the sugar.

Add the lime leaves and lemongrass stick.

Add loads of ice, then top with soda water to taste.

Stir with the lemongrass stick and serve.

PIMM'S

This is a classic English summertime drink and a wonderful way to start a barbecue. It celebrates the best things about an English summer: strawberries, cool cucumbers and the slight bitterness of the Pimm's — or is that just the taste left in the Poms' mouths from losing at the cricket!

Pimm's is one of those drinks that goes with most food, but its cooling effect particularly suits spicy dishes. I like to have it with Peri-peri chicken (page 167).

MAKES 2 LITRES (8 CUPS)

100 g strawberries, halved or quartered

1 orange, sliced

1 lemon, sliced

1 large apple, diced

½ cucumber, sliced

ice cubes

500 ml (2 cups) Pimm's

1.5 litres (6 cups) lemonade

1 cup mint

Combine the fruit and cucumber with plenty of ice in a large jug or punch bowl.

Pour in the Pimm's and lemonade.

Stir to mix, then add the mint.

Serve straight away.

SOUTHERN CROSS PIMM'S

I love this combination — it's such a cool, refreshing mix — though I think this is probably the only way one should ever ingest the New Zealand fruit feijoas. That's why I call this cocktail the Southern Cross Pimm's!

You need to watch out for this one: it grabs you and takes you on a journey!

SERVES 1

ice cubes

1 cucumber, cut into thin slices or sticks

¼ lime

mint leaves

50 ml Feijoa Vodka (made by 42 Below)

lemonade

Place plenty of ice cubes in a glass, along with the cucumber, lime (give it a squeeze) and some mint leaves.

Pour over the vodka, top with lemonade and stir.

Serve straight away.

DARK AND STORMY

This Cuban concoction is a cocktail classic, generally made with dark rum. It's a fantastic mix of spicy ginger beer, sweet dark rum and sour lime that's perfect on a hot summer's day and goes down a treat with spicy Jerked chicken (page 164) or some finger-licking Classic barbecued sticky ribs (page 152).

SERVES 1

½ lime

crushed ice

50 ml dark rum

100 ml ginger beer

lime slices

Squeeze the lime over crushed ice.

Pour over the rum and ginger beer.

Garnish with a few lime slices and stir.

MARGARITA

While filming a television series in Perth, we found ourselves discussing the merits of good tequila. Levon, one of the crew, boasted that he had, and I quote, 'the best margarita recipe in the world'. Well, Levon, it's pretty damned good, so I have paid it homage by including it here for all to try. I think I prefer mine shaken over ice and strained but you can try it as you like — frozen or just over ice, it's bloody good.

This mix can make as much or as little as you like. It's pretty straightforward: for two drinks, use 60 ml (¼ cup) of alcohol and then do the maths. If you want a frozen margarita, fill the glasses with ice to measure, then blitz the ice with the booze in a blender and pour it back into the glasses. For a chilled drink, just shake the alcohol with the ice and strain it back into the glasses.

SERVES 2

30 ml gold tequila

15 ml silver tequila

15 ml Cointreau

juice of 1 lime

15 ml lime cordial

pinch of salt

crushed ice

Combine the liquids and pinch of salt in a shaker or blender, depending on whether you are making chilled or frozen drinks.

Measure the ice to fill each glass and add to the shaker or blender. For chilled drinks, just use the ice from one glass.

Shake or blend the cocktail until thoroughly mixed and divide betweenthe glasses.

If making chilled drinks, dip the rims in fine table salt before pouring the cocktail.

SAUCES
and
RUBS

BASIC BARBECUE SAUCE	MEXICAN SPICY GREEN SAUCE
BAJA SAUCE	**SWEET CHILLI SAUCE**
SATAY SAUCE	THAI SWEET CHILLI JAM
SALSA VERDE	**NAM PRIK PLA**
ORANGE AND GINGER KETCHUP	NUOC CHAM
ANCHOVY AND ROSEMARY SAUCE	**MASTER STOCK**
HARISSA	MAYONNAISE
AVOCADO PESTO	**BASIL MAYONNAISE**
HOT CHILLI SAUCE	AÏOLI
SALSA DI DRAGONCELLO	**COMPOUND BUTTERS: HERB BUTTER**
CHIMICHURRI	COMPOUND BUTTERS: CAFÉ DE PARIS
ERBE SALSA PICANTE	**COMPOUND BUTTERS: CAJUN**
HOISIN DIPPING SAUCE	CAJUN SPICE
GUACAMOLE	**SMOKED SALT AND ROSEMARY**
SHALLOT AND CORIANDER SALSA	CLASSIC BARBECUE RIB RUB
SWEET CORN, BLACK GARLIC AND CORIANDER SALSA	**GARLIC, LEMON AND GREEN PEPPERCORN SALT**
SSAMJANG	CELERY SALT
MISO MARINADE	**CHIPOTLE SALT**

BASIC BARBECUE SAUCE

MAKES 485 G

1 cup dark brown sugar

250 ml (1 cup) sherry vinegar (preferably aged)

1 onion, chopped

1 teaspoon ground cumin

½ teaspoon ground cinnamon

1 star anise

1 jalapeño chilli, halved

2 teaspoons smoked paprika

60 ml (¼ cup) tomato ketchup

200 g tinned chopped tomatoes

1 tablespoon salt

No self-respecting American pit master would be caught behind a barbecue without a barbecue sauce recipe, and this one's both a sauce and a glaze. I brush it over barbecued ribs or pork belly in the final stages of cooking to create a glaze, but you can also use it as a straight barbecue sauce with grilled meats or sausages.

This basic recipe is a simple combination of sweet and sour components that works really well. If you'd like to try something a little different, experiment with fruit juices and other spices to mix it up a little. It's all about personal tastes.

Combine all the ingredients in a heavy-bottomed saucepan.

Bring to the boil, then reduce to a low simmer and cook for 30 minutes.

Use a stick blender to puree until the sauce is smooth. If the sauce is still thin, continue to cook it until the sauce coats the back of a spoon well.

Serve at room temperature. The sauce will keep for up to 3 months in the refrigerator if stored in an airtight container.

BAJA
SAUCE

This sauce is great served with Mexican suckling pig tortillas (page 148) as an alternative to Mexican spicy green sauce (page 269), or dolloped on Baked sweet potatoes (page 56) — just about anything where you want chilli, but not the heat of the Hot chilli sauce (page 263).

MAKES ABOUT
125 G (½ CUP)

100 g sour cream

1 tablespoon Hot chilli sauce (page 263)

juice of 1 lime

salt, to taste

Combine all the ingredients together and mix well.

This sauce is best used when made as the dairy element means that it will spoil after a few days.

SATAY
SAUCE

This is quite possibly the best sauce ever invented for barbecued foods!

MAKES 500 ML
(2 CUPS)

½ large onion, chopped

1 lemongrass stem, white part only, chopped

2 teaspoons chilli powder

2 tablespoons oil

320 g (2 cups) roasted peanuts, ground in a food processor

400 ml can coconut milk

1 tablespoon tamarind paste

1½ tablespoons sugar

salt, to taste

Puree the onion, lemongrass and chilli powder together in a food processor to a fine paste.

Heat the oil in a saucepan and fry the puree for about 5 minutes, until fragrant.

Stir in the roasted ground peanuts, coconut milk, tamarind paste and sugar, and bring the boil.

Simmer until the sauce is thick and season with salt.

Serve warm. You can keep the remaining sauce in the refrigerator for at least two weeks – it wll set firm but reheats well, just add a little water to avoid splitting.

SALSA VERDE

MAKES 300 ML

1 cup flat-leaf or curly parsley

1 cup basil

1 cup mint

1 cup rocket

2 tablespoons capers

6 anchovy fillets

1 garlic clove, peeled

1½ tablespoons good quality
white wine vinegar

2 teaspoons dijon mustard

185 ml good quality extra virgin olive oil

freshly ground black pepper

salt

This all-time classic Italian sauce pairs perfectly with grilled meat, fish, poultry and vegetables. Key elements are really good extra virgin olive oil, fresh herbs and good vinegar; you can also use lemon juice.

A tip for making a great salsa verde is to use a sharp knife or to have a sharp blade in your food processor, so the herbs are cut and not bruised.

Place the herbs in a food processor with the capers, anchovies and garlic, and process until finely chopped. If necessary, add the vinegar to loosen the mixture.

Spoon the mixture into a bowl and stir in the mustard and olive oil. Combine completely, then season with pepper and salt.

Allow the salsa to stand for 30 minutes before using. Serve at room temperature.

The sauce will keep for up to a week in the refrigerator if stored in an airtight container.

ORANGE AND GINGER KETCHUP

One of my sous chefs came up with this great variation on that old favourite tomato ketchup. It's great with barbecued duck, in particular, and also with scallops or prawns. Historically, tomato ketchup is a Chinese sauce that was popularised by the Americans, so this combo makes a lot of sense.

MAKES 250 ML (1 CUP)

250 ml (1 cup) tomato ketchup

zest and strained juice of 1 orange

1 teaspoon finely chopped fresh ginger

½ teaspoon dark sesame oil

Combine the ketchup with the orange zest and juice. Add the ginger and sesame oil, and mix thoroughly.

Allow the sauce to stand for 30 minutes before using.

Use this sauce on the same day.

ANCHOVY AND ROSEMARY SAUCE

I first came across the recipe for this Italian sauce at the River Café in London, and it epitomises the simple, big flavours of Italian cooking. It is the perfect accompaniment to grilled meat and fish, and absolutely wonderful on vegetables, especially broccoli and asparagus. I also like to use it as a rub for roasting legs of lamb, but with a lot less olive oil.

In my experience, people who don't normally like anchovies find this recipe a great introduction to their flavour, as the balance of lemon and rosemary diminishes the fishiness. Give it a go, you will love it!

SERVES 4

8 anchovy fillets, rinsed

juice of 2 lemons

½ teaspoon finely chopped rosemary

160 ml extra virgin olive oil

Pound or chop the anchovy fillets into a paste.

Mix in the lemon juice to make a creamy paste, then add the rosemary.

Spoon in the olive oil to create a semi-emulsion.

This sauce is best used straight away. It will keep for up to 3 days in the refrigerator if stored in an airtight container.

HARISSA

Harissa originates from Tunisia, but is commonly found throughout North Africa. It is a wonderful condiment to accompany barbecued lamb, or Lamb kofte (page 154), and goes well with grilled fish. Harissa also makes a great marinade for chicken and oily fish like mackerel, and is used to make salad dressings.

MAKES 160 G

½ teaspoon cumin seeds

1 teaspoon sea salt

1 large garlic clove, peeled

5 long red chillies, roughly chopped

2 tablespoons white wine vinegar

1 tablespoon extra virgin olive oil

Place the cumin seeds and salt in a mortar and pound to combine.

Add the garlic and pound to a paste.

Add the chopped chillies and continue pounding.

Pour in the vinegar, followed by the olive oil, and pound until combined.

This sauce is best used straight away. It will keep for up to 1 week if refrigerated in an airtight container. When re-using, allow the sauce to come back to room temperature.

AVOCADO PESTO

This is a fabulous, healthy dip to serve while everyone is mingling prior to the main event. Being based on avocado, you don't have to use olive oil in this pesto. Hass avocados work well in this dip.

SERVES 4–6

2 ripe avocados

½ cup pine nuts, or 1 cup cashew nuts, lightly toasted

1 cup grated parmesan

2 cups sweet basil

juice of 1 lemon

salt

freshly ground black pepper

flour tortillas, lightly toasted on the barbecue

Peel the avocado and put the flesh in a food processor, along with the nuts, cheese and basil. Blend until smooth.

Add the lemon juice, and salt and pepper to taste. Transfer to a small bowl.

Break your toasted tortillas into shards and serve around the avocado pesto.

As with most avocado products, this pesto will oxidise if left uncovered – it does not affect the flavour, just the appearance. To avoid this, cover with a thin layer of olive oil or just eat it all soon after making!

HOT
CHILLI
SAUCE

I love this sauce! When my habanero plant is in full fruit I make jars of this stuff and give it to friends. It's absolutely awesome and hot, and perfect for any barbecue — put it in your bloody Mary for an extra kick.

I also mix it with sour cream to make Baja sauce (page 259), which is great on hotdogs and Mexican foods.

MAKES 500 ML (2 CUPS)

1 tablespoon vegetable oil

1 small onion, chopped

2 garlic cloves, chopped

1 cup chopped carrot

10 habanero chillies

60 ml (¼ cup) lime juice

60 ml (¼ cup) white vinegar

1 teaspoon English mustard

1 teaspoon salt

250 ml (1 cup) water

Heat the oil in a frying pan over low heat. Gently sauté the onion and garlic until soft but not coloured.

Add the remaining ingredients and simmer until the carrot is soft.

Place the mixture in a blender. Don't worry if you think the mixture is too watery — it needs to have a bit of liquid. Blend until smooth. This sauce will keep for several months in a clean, airtight container.

SALSA
DI
DRAGONCELLO

For me, this is like a béarnaise sauce, only a lot better for you! It is fantastic with boiled meats, fish and vegetables, and would be perfect served with Bistecca alla fiorentina (page 184) or any barbecued steak.

MAKES 300 G

6 eggs

100 g stale ciabatta (2–3 days old), crust removed

60 ml (¼ cup) white wine vinegar

1 cup chopped tarragon

6 anchovy fillets, chopped

1 tablespoon chopped salted capers

salt

freshly ground black pepper

120 ml extra virgin olive oil

Put the eggs in a saucepan of cold water, bring to the boil and simmer for 10 minutes, or until hard-boiled. Place the eggs under running cold water until cool enough to handle, then shell them. Discard the egg whites and chop the yolks.

Soak the stale bread in a little warm water until soft. Add the vinegar, and once the bread is soft, squeeze the excess moisture and mash with a fork to break it up.

Add the tarragon, anchovies, capers and egg yolks, and combine. Season with salt and pepper, then add the olive oil. Allow to rest for 20–30 minutes before using.

This sauce is best used straight away, served at room temperature. It will keep for 2 days in the refrigerator if stored in an airtight container.

CHIMICHURRI

MAKES 250 ML (1 CUP)

1 tablespoon dried wild oregano flowers or dried oregano

2 tablespoons finely chopped oregano or sweet marjoram

3 garlic cloves, finely chopped

3 shallots, finely chopped

½ teaspoon chilli flakes

½ teaspoon coarsely ground black pepper

60 ml (¼ cup) white wine vinegar

120 ml extra virgin olive oil

salt

This South American barbecue sauce is used right across the continent, from the southern Pampas region to as far north as Honduras. It has as many variations as, say, the Italian salsa verde, but in its purest form it is just dried oregano, vinegar, chilli flakes, black pepper and olive oil. I like to use a combination of fresh and dried herbs because of their different characteristics.

In South America this recipe is used specifically for grilled meats (i.e. the perfect steak), but you can also spoon it liberally over chicken or fish. The South Americans don't go in for fancy rubs and marinades — it's all about the MEAT.

If possible, use dried wild oregano flowers to make this sauce — they're far more aromatic than just oregano leaves.

Rub the oregano flowers between your fingers to break them up. Combine with the chopped fresh herbs.

Add the garlic, shallots, chilli flakes and pepper. Pour in the vinegar, combine and let stand for 10 minutes.

Stir in the olive oil and season with salt to taste.

This sauce is best used straight away, as the acidity of the vinegar overpowers the freshness of the herb flavours if kept for too long.

ERBE SALSA
PICANTE

I love adding this terrific herb salsa to add to grilled meat and fish, and any slowly barbecued meats that have a rich intense flavour, like short ribs. This is a fresh salsa and won't keep for more than a day, so use it liberally!

SERVES 10

1 large red onion, very finely diced

3 long dried red chillies (more if you like heat)

1 garlic clove, chopped

1 tablespoon chopped marjoram

½ cup mint

½ cup sweet basil

1 tablespoon dried oregano

2 tablespoons red wine vinegar

salt

freshly cracked black pepper

80 ml (⅓ cup) extra virgin olive oil

Combine the onion, dried chillies, garlic and all the fresh and dried herbs.

Add the vinegar and mix well. Season with salt and pepper to taste. Loosen with the olive oil.

Transfer to a bowl and serve straight away.

HOISIN DIPPING SAUCE

This dipping sauce is usually served with rice paper rolls, but I also love it with the Best ever crispy roast pork belly (page 169)!

MAKES ABOUT 1¼ CUPS

125 ml (½ cup) hoisin sauce

60 ml (¼ cup) rice wine vinegar

½ cup toasted cashew nuts, finely ground

Combine the hoisin and vinegar and mix well. Stir in the ground cashews.

If the sauce is very thick, thin it out with a little water.

Serve drizzled over dishes, or in a sauce dish on the side. This sauce will keep for at least a week – but you'll probably use it all before then anyway!

GUACAMOLE

This salsa goes so well with barbecued pork or chicken, and especially with spicy food. It's the perfect accompaniment to the adobo-marinated Mexican suckling pig tortillas (page 148). You can also serve it as a dip with plain tortillas or as a general addition to your barbecue.

I think the creamy flesh of dark-skinned Hass avocados is best suited to making guacamole. Ripe red tomatoes are fine for this recipe if good green varieties are unavailable.

SERVES 4

2 Hass avocados, halved, peeled and stone removed

1 jalapeño chilli, seeded and chopped

juice of 2 limes

2 shallots, finely diced

1 green tomato, seeded and chopped

1 tablespoon chopped coriander leaves and stems

salt

freshly ground black pepper

Roughly mash the avocados with a fork.

Add the remaining ingredients and roughly combine.

Guacamole is best served straight away. It won't go off if you keep it for a day or two in the refrigerator, but it may change colour to an unpleasant brown!

SHALLOT AND CORIANDER SALSA

This is the Mexican equivalent of an Indian raita, and makes a refreshing antidote to the heat of some of the chilli sauces served with a Mexican barbacoa. I serve this with my Mexican suckling pig tortillas (page 148), but it's equally good with the Whole fish Thai style (page 95) or Barbecued pepper chicken curry (page 172).

MAKES 200 G

2 cups finely sliced white salad onion

2 tablespoons chopped coriander leaves

1 green capsicum (pepper), finely diced

juice of 1 lime

freshly ground black pepper

Combine the onions, coriander and capsicum.

Squeeze the lime juice over the salsa and season with a pinch of pepper.

Serve straight away, as this salsa doesn't keep well.

SWEET CORN, BLACK GARLIC AND CORIANDER SALSA

Black garlic, or fermented garlic, is a relatively new product available in gourmet delis and some of the major supermarkets. The fermentation process converts the sugars in the garlic to change the flavour from a harsh and peppery to a sticky black, slightly sharp, less aggressive garlic flavour. It's full of antioxidants, but its soft sticky texture is what makes it so good! It's great in salads and can also be mashed up and used to make aioli for something different. There is no substitute really, so keep an eye out for it.

Prepare your barbecue for cooking over a medium heat.

Cook the corn on the barbecue, turning occasionally, for 30 minutes, until lightly charred and cooked through. Remove from the barbecue and leave to cool.

Meanwhile, if using the dried ancho chilli, toast the whole chilli in a frying pan over high heat for 1–2 minutes, until it puffs up. Remove the stem and seeds. Soak the chilli in boiling water for 5 minutes, until soft. Drain and pat dry, then thinly slice into strips. (If using fresh chilli, just add it to the salad below.)

Peel the husks from the corn. Cut off the kernels and add to a bowl with the tomatoes, onion and black garlic.

Toss with the chilli, coriander, lime juice, olive oil, and salt and pepper to taste. Transfer to a serving dish.

This salsa is best used with in one to two days – the black garlic can dominate the flavour of the salsa if left too long.

SERVES 4–6

3 corn cobs, in their husks

1 dried ancho chilli, or 1 thinly sliced long red fresh chilli

200 g cherry tomatoes, halved

1 red onion, halved and thinly sliced

1 small tub (50–80 g) peeled black garlic, quartered

1 cup coriander leaves

juice of 1 lime

2 tablespoons extra virgin olive oil

salt

freshly ground black pepper

SSAMJANG

A Korean staple, ssamjang is a sauce made from a mixture of kochujang, a chilli pepper paste, and dwenjang, a fermented soya bean paste. Both pastes are available from Korean supermarkets or speciality Asian stores, and you can also buy ssamjang ready-made. It is used as a condiment with barbecued meats, which are then wrapped in lettuce with fresh herbs, and it can be added to stir-fries or used as a marinade or ribs. I use this sauce to accompany Daegi bulgogi: spicy Korean pork (page 168). Place all the ingredients in a food processor and puree until smooth.

MAKES 425 G

80 ml (⅓ cup) kochujang

125 ml (½ cup) dwenjang

1 tablespoon finely chopped bird's eye chilli

1 tablespoon finely chopped green pepper
or capsicum (pepper)

6 garlic cloves, peeled

2 teaspoons sesame seeds

2 tablespoons rice wine vinegar

1 tablespoon sesame oil

This sauce will keep for up to 3 weeks in the refrigerator if stored in an airtight container.

MISO MARINADE

This recipe is both a base for sauces and dressings, and a marinade for fish and chicken. Add it to Mayonnaise (page 272) or combine with wasabi, rice vinegar and oil for a fantastic dressing. This marinade is used in the Miso-blackened fish fillets (page 102) and robatayaki-style Miso eggplant (page 44).

MAKES 500 G

500 g white miso paste

250 ml (1 cup) mirin

½ cup caster sugar

Combine the ingredients and place the mixture in a glass bowl suspended over a simmering saucepan of water. Leave it to cook for 1 hour, until the sugar has completely dissolved.

Allow to cool, then use as a marinade.

The marinade will keep for up to 1 month in the refrigerator if stored in an airtight container. It also freezes really well.

MEXICAN SPICY GREEN SAUCE

The recipe for this great sauce was given to me by a Mexican waiter at Monte's in London when I was head chef there. I use it to accompany Mexican barbecue dishes, such as Mexican suckling pig tortillas (page 148). It also works well when strained and served with raw fish as a dipping sauce.

MAKES 250 ML (1 CUP)

4 shallots

4 green chillies, seeded

100 ml lime juice

100 ml white wine vinegar or rice vinegar

2 tablespoons chopped coriander leaves

1 garlic clove, peeled

Combine all the ingredients in a food processor and puree into a medium-textured sauce.

Use straight away. This sauce can't be stored for too long as the colour starts to fade after a few hours.

SWEET CHILLI SAUCE

Sweet chilli sauce exploded onto the food scene and became a gastro-pub staple served with chunky chips and sour cream. It shows how versatile the sauce is, and how popular it has become. It's the perfect accompaniment to Gai yang: Thai barbecued chicken (page 214), and also works well with barbecued seafood — prawns, scallops or lobster.

If you prefer a milder sauce, use eight rather than fifteen chillies!

MAKES 600 ML

500 g caster sugar

500 ml (2 cups) white wine vinegar

500 ml (2 cups) water

4 lemongrass stems, white part only, finely sliced

10 garlic cloves, peeled

15 long red chillies, chopped

½ teaspoon salt

Combine the sugar, vinegar and water in a saucepan and bring to the boil.

Place the lemongrass, garlic, chillies and salt in a food processor and puree to a fine paste.

Add the paste to the saucepan, then simmer and reduce by half. Skim off any floating bits or any foam that forms.

Once thickened, set aside to cool.

The sauce will keep for up to 2 months in the refrigerator if stored in an airtight container.

THAI SWEET CHILLI JAM

This sophisticated version of sweet chilli sauce is fantastic served with grilled scallops and prawns or smeared over barbecued fish or pork ribs. It's somewhat complicated to make but worth the effort.

MAKES 535 G

500 ml (2 cups) sunflower oil

125 g garlic, sliced lengthwise

250 g red Asian shallots, sliced lengthwise

½ cup dried shrimp, rinsed in hot water and drained

8 dried long red chillies

125 g palm sugar

75 g tamarind paste

1 tablespoon fish sauce

salt

Heat 375 ml of the oil in a wok or large saucepan. Fry the garlic and shallots separately until lightly golden, then remove and drain. Be careful, as they will continue to cook and darken once removed from the oil.

Fry the shrimp and chillies until fragrant, then remove and drain. Puree the fried ingredients with the remaining oil to form a paste. Transfer to a saucepan and bring to the boil.

Add the palm sugar, tamarind paste and fish sauce. Season with salt and simmer for 2–3 minutes until thick. The sauce will keep for up to 1 week in the refrigerator if stored in an airtight container.

NAM PRIK PLA

This simple Thai condiment is very versatile and can be used as a dipping sauce or dressing. It's great with Smoked beef short ribs (page 221) and dishes such as Pickled cucumber, mint and chilli salad (page 85).

SERVES 10

100 ml fish sauce

100 ml lime juice

3 bird's eye chillies (more if you like heat)

3 red Asian shallots, finely diced

1 tablespoon palm sugar

2 garlic cloves, sliced

Combine all the ingredients and serve.

Use straight away so the flavours are fresh and the shallots are crunchy. After a while the shallots become soft and the colours leach together.

NUOC CHAM

This dipping sauce tastes absolutely fantastic and adds a light sweet–sour flavour to Vietnamese barbecued dishes. It's traditionally used as a dressing for most Vietnamese salads.

MAKES 250 ML
(1 CUP)

5 tablespoons caster sugar

60 ml (¼ cup) water

80 ml (⅓ cup) fish sauce

juice of 3 limes

1 large or 2 small garlic cloves, finely crushed

1 long red chilli, or 2 bird's eye chillies if you like heat

Whisk the sugar with the water.

Add the fish sauce and lime juice, and stir to dissolve the sugar completely.

Add the garlic and chilli and combine.

Allow the sauce to rest for 1 hour before serving.

The sauce will keep for up to 2 weeks in the refrigerator if stored in an airtight container.

MASTER STOCK

This master stock can be stored for an indefinite period in an airtight container in the fridge. Just boil it for about 5 minutes prior to each use.

MAKES ABOUT
1 LITRE
(4 CUPS)

300 ml dark soy sauce

250 ml light soy sauce

100 ml shaoxing rice wine

100 g rock sugar (available from Chinese grocers — using this sugar makes all the difference!)

3 star anise

1 cinnamon stick

1 dried long chilli

2 pieces dried mandarin peel

6 slices fresh ginger

6 spring onions, trimmed

500 ml (2 cups) water

Combine all the ingredients in a large saucepan and simmer until the sugar has dissolved.

Let stand until cool so the flavours steep and then you can use it as a marinade or a cure for meats. There is no need to strain.

Store in an air-tight container in the refrigerator until required. The master stock can be frozen if not required for some time.

MAYONNAISE

**MAKES
600 ML**

3 large egg yolks

salt

2 teaspoons dijon mustard

1 teaspoon white wine vinegar

1 teaspoon water

500 ml (2 cups) vegetable oil
or extra virgin olive oil

freshly ground black pepper

juice of ½ lemon

Where would we be without this staple dressing for most backyard barbecues? Mayonnaise is just perfect on a burger, in a potato salad — you name it, this popular dressing can find a home on anything. But mayonnaise can be so much more than the white creamy dressing we all know and love. Different oils can take it in different directions and any number of other ingredients can be added to it to lift it to greater glory.

The type of oil you use depends on how you want to use the mayonnaise. Extra virgin olive oil will give you a powerful taste that might not suit the subtle flavours of some fish, for example. Again, it comes down to personal taste.

I love to serve the basil mayo with barbecued fish. You could also use it in Coleslaw (page 74) instead of Greek yoghurt.

Place the egg yolks, a good pinch of salt, the mustard, vinegar and 1 teaspoon water in a bowl. Whisk to combine and aerate for 1–2 minutes.

Wet a tea towel, then roll it up and wind it around the base of the bowl to secure it, leaving your hands free to whisk and pour.

Pour the oil into the egg mixture in a thin but steady stream, whisking continuously. Stop for a little if your hand and arm become tired. Continue pouring and whisking until all the oil is added.

If the mixture is thick and too gluggy, thin it with a little water.

Season the mayonnaise with salt and pepper and a squeeze of lemon juice.

Use straight away. Any leftover mayo will keep for 1 week in the refrigerator if stored in an airtight container.

BASIL
MAYONNAISE

MAKES 600 ML
---

1 cup basil

pinch of salt

1 quantity Mayonnaise (previous page),
made with extra virgin olive oil

squeeze of lemon juice

Pound the basil with the salt to form a fine paste,
then add to the mayonnaise and stir.

Correct the seasoning with a squeeze of lemon juice.

AIOLI

MAKES 600 ML
---

3 garlic cloves, peeled

pinch of salt

1 quantity Mayonnaise (previous page)

squeeze of lemon juice

Pound the garlic with the salt to form a paste.

Combine the garlic with the mayonnaise and correct
the seasoning with a squeeze of lemon juice.

COMPOUND BUTTERS: HERB BUTTER

MAKES ABOUT 600 G

500 g unsalted butter, at room temperature

2 tablespoons chopped dill

2 tablespoons chopped chives

2 tablespoons chopped flat-leaf parsley

2 small garlic cloves, finely chopped

80 ml (⅓ cup) cognac

Compound butters are a great way to use up extra herbs or seasonings, and add flavour and moisture to barbecued meat, fish or vegetables. Once made they keep for up to three months in the freezer. In London, when the truffles were at their best and cheapest, we would buy loads and make butter and freeze it – then we would have truffle butter for pasta, steaks and chicken for months. You can make all types of compound butters – you're only limited by your imagination.

Whip the softened butter until light and fluffy, using the balloon whisk attachment of an electric mixer.

Add the remaining ingredients and combine well by whisking slowly.

Once well combined, transfer the butter mixture onto a sheet of foil, lined with baking paper.

Shape the butter into a thick sausage, then fold the paper and foil over. Tighten into a solid sausage shape and twist the ends to seal.

Place in the freezer to harden.

To use, simply cut off some butter discs with a sharp knife, then unwrap them.

Allow to soften at room temperature, then serve on top of hot grilled meat or seafood, such as Grilled lobsters (page 100).

The butter will keep in the freezer for several months.

COMPOUND BUTTERS: CAFÉ DE PARIS

MAKES ABOUT 600 G

500 g unsalted butter, at room temperature

1 tablespoon dijon mustard

1 tablespoon chopped dill

1 tablespoon chopped tarragon

1 tablespoon chopped flat-leaf parsley

2 tablespoons very finely chopped shallots

1 garlic clove, finely chopped

1 teaspoon curry powder

1 teaspoon smoked paprika

3 anchovy fillets, finely chopped

1 tablespoon worcestershire sauce

Whip the softened butter until light and fluffy, using the balloon whisk attachment of an electric mixer.

Add the remaining ingredients and combine well by whisking slowly.

Once well combined, transfer the butter mixture onto a sheet of foil, lined with baking paper.

Shape the butter into a thick sausage, then fold the paper and foil over. Tighten into a solid sausage shape and twist the ends to seal. Place in the freezer to harden.

To use, simply cut off some butter discs with a sharp knife, then unwrap them.

Allow to soften at room temperature, then serve on top of hot grilled meat or seafood.

The butter will keep in the freezer for several months.

COMPOUND BUTTERS: CAJUN

MAKES ABOUT 600 G

500 g unsalted butter, at room temperature

1 onion, very finely chopped

2 jalapeño chillies, seeded and very finely chopped

1 cup chopped coriander leaves and stems

3 tablespoons Cajun spice (page 276)

Whip the softened butter until light and fluffy, using the balloon whisk attachment of an electric mixer.

Add the remaining ingredients and combine well by whisking slowly.

Once well combined, transfer the butter mixture onto a sheet of foil, lined with baking paper.

Shape the butter into a thick sausage, then fold the paper and foil over. Tighten into a solid sausage shape and twist the ends to seal.

Place in the freezer to harden.

To use, simply cut off some butter discs with a sharp knife, then unwrap them.

Allow to soften at room temperature, then serve on top of hot grilled meat or seafood.

The butter will keep in the freezer for several months.

CAJUN SPICE

MAKES 130 G

500 ml (2 cups) sunflower oil

1 large onion, finely sliced

10 garlic cloves, finely sliced

1 tablespoon cayenne pepper

1 tablespoon smoked paprika

1 tablespoon Celery salt (page 279)

1 tablespoon dried thyme

1 teaspoon fennel seeds

Cajun food was the big thing when I was an apprentice chef in the late 1980s, and we used to make our own spice mixture. We'd mix it with flour to deep-fry squid, dredge fish fillets through it prior to pan-frying and rub it onto pork. I particularly like to use this recipe as a base to make a rub for pork ribs or pork belly. Mix three parts Cajun spice to one part sugar and one part salt, then rub it all over the meat.

When I'm making dried herbs, I like to pick or buy fresh herbs then tie them together at their stems and hang them up to dry. Once they are dry, place them in an airtight container and they will last for up to a month. It's a great way to get the most out of your herbs.

Heat the oil in a wok. It needs to be hot! It should be about 150°C, or able to cook a slice of bread to a golden colour in 20 seconds.

Cook the onion and garlic separately, moving them around constantly so they cook evenly. Remove them from the heat when they start to turn a light golden colour, and place them on paper towel to cool and drain. You'll notice they will continue to colour.

Place the cooled fried onion and garlic in a hand-held food processor, along with the remaining ingredients, and blitz to a rough powder.

The spice will keep for 1 month if stored in an airtight container.

Cajun rub

Add 1 tablespoon soft brown sugar or palm sugar and 1 tablespoon salt to 3 tablespoons Cajun spice. Rub into the meat you are using and allow to marinate. The length of marinating time depends on the size of the joint or meat to be cooked; steaks or pork fillets will need 10–15 minutes, ribs maybe 30 minutes, and a beef brisket will need to be marinated overnight.

SMOKED SALT AND ROSEMARY

Whoever thought of smoking salt was a smart cookie. When wet, salt absorbs flavours really well and, depending on the wood you use, you can achieve an aggressive flavour or a subtle one. Smoked salt gives a great boost to a grilled piece of meat and you can also use it as a straight substitute for normal salt in your rub recipes. Once you have experienced good smoked salt you will find it hard to season meat with anything else!

Smoking salt is a really cool process, but you'll need to use a kettle-type barbecue or a hooded gas one. You'll also need to pre-soak your woodchips in water for an hour.

I love this combination of smoke and rosemary. Rosemary is an oily herb and easy to dry at home. I think you get a better flavour from home-dried herbs, so have a crack at this combination! Just tie fresh rosemary together at the stems and hang it up to dry. It will keep for up to a month if stored in an airtight container.

Wet the salt a little, so it is damp but not slushy.

Prepare your barbecue so you have a small area of indirect heat to one side. If using a gas barbecue, just turn one burner on. Place the salt on the barbecue, away from the heat source.

Add 1 cup of pre-soaked woodchips to the heat source, or smoke box if using gas, and once you have a good smoke going place the lid on the barbecue. Smoke for about 1 hour, adding woodchips as required.

Allow the salt to cool, then mix with the home-dried rosemary.

The salt will keep for 1 month if stored in an airtight container or reusable grinder.

MAKES 200 G

2 cups coarse rock salt

4 cups hickory or mesquite woodchips

½ cup home-dried rosemary

CLASSIC BARBECUE RIB RUB

We owe the Americans a great deal of thanks when it comes to barbecuing and the use of rubs. Pork has always been the mainstay of the American barbecue (well, except in Texas) and the rub is what defines a great piece of barbecued pork, along with a good deal of smoke and love. Whether it's ribs, belly, shoulder, neck or cutlets — you name it, pork loves this treatment.

MAKES ENOUGH FOR 1 SHOULDER OF PORK, 1 BELLY OR 3–4 RIB RACKS

3 tablespoons smoked paprika

6 tablespoons soft brown sugar

1 tablespoon Chipotle salt (page opposite)

2 tablespoons Celery salt (page opposite)

1 teaspoon ground ginger

2 teaspoons whole black peppercorns

1 teaspoon mustard powder

1 teaspoon onion flakes

1 teaspoon garlic flakes

Place all the ingredients in a small food processor and grind until fine. You could also use a mortar and pestle.

The rub will keep for 1 month if stored in an airtight container.

GARLIC LEMON AND GREEN PEPPERCORN SALT

The great thing about salt is that it absorbs flavours so well. I fell in love with the practice of making my own salt when I was running the kitchen at Monte's in London, as sometimes it's nice to have something a bit different to grind onto a piece of fish or meat before you throw it onto the coals. Try this seasoning on Bender's beer-can chicken (page 175) roasted on the barbecue, whole grilled fish or whatever takes your fancy!

MAKES 150 G

4 garlic cloves, thinly sliced

1 unwaxed lemon, thinly sliced

10 dried lemon verbena leaves

1 tablespoon dried green peppercorns

1 cup coarse rock salt

Line a baking tray with baking paper. Arrange the slices of garlic and lemon on the baking paper, making sure they are lying flat.

Place the tray in a 100°C oven and leave to dry until crisp. This may take 1 hour for the garlic, and up to 2 hours for the lemon.

Break the dried lemon and garlic into a bowl, along with the lemon verbena leaves.

Roughly crush the green peppercorns and add to the bowl.

Add enough salt to achieve an equal amount of dried ingredients and salt, and combine well.

The salt will keep for 1 month if stored in an airtight container or reusable grinder.

CELERY
SALT

This is one of my favourite flavoured salts. It's a great way to use up all those dark green celery leaves that most people throw away. Celery salt adds wonderful flavour to fish, poultry and grilled meats, and it's also superb in rub recipes. I make a legendary Bloody Mary thanks to this secret ingredient!

When making any flavoured salt, it's imperative that you start with a top-quality salt. I always use coarse rock salt.

MAKES 165 G

2 cups dark celery leaves

approximately 1 cup good quality coarse rock salt

1 teaspoon celery seeds (optional)

Wash the celery leaves and spin dry or allow to drain well.

Place the leaves in a large mortar, along with ½ cup of the salt. Use a grinding motion to form a paste, which may be quite wet at first.

Add up to a ¼ cup more salt and grind until the paste is just moist and the leaves are well ground into the salt; you may not need to add the remaining ¼ cup of salt. The salt should be a nice pale to medium green colour, depending on the darkness of the leaves.

Line a baking tray with baking paper. If using the celery seeds, add them to the salt. Spread the mix evenly over the baking paper and place in a 100°C oven for around 1 hour, until completely dry.

The salt will keep for 1 month if stored in an airtight container or reusable grinder.

CHIPOTLE
SALT

This funky salt works well in rubs and as a seasoning. You get the heat of the jalapeño chilli plus a smoky flavour, because chipotles are smoked jalapeño chillies!

This salt is great on steaks, fish or pork, or for seasoning your classic adobo marinade for Mexican suckling pig tortillas (page 148).

MAKES 250 G

8 chipotle chillies

1 cup coarse rock salt

Toast the chipotle chillies in a hot frying pan for 1–2 minutes. Remove the stems and seeds, then soak the chillies in 250 ml (1 cup) boiling water for 10 minutes.

Drain, then place the chillies in a large mortar, along with ½ cup of the salt, and grind to a rough paste. Add the remaining salt and grind a little more.

Line a baking tray with baking paper. Spread the salt evenly over the baking paper and place in a 100°C oven for around 1 hour, until completely dry.

The salt will keep for 1 month if stored in an airtight container.

CHEF'S NOTES

Most ingredients in this book can be bought from general supermarkets or specialty stores. I always try to buy the best ingredients I can afford, which doesn't mean that everything always has to be organic or that meat needs to be sourced from rare breeds reared by monks in virgin forests! But if it's possible for me to buy the best, I will.

CHEESE Cheese, whether parmesan or cheddar, is always freshly grated.

CHICKEN Chicken is preferably free range and organic.

CITRUS Lemon zest or citrus zest is finely grated.

CREAM Cream is generally pouring cream with a fat content of 35%.

EGGS Eggs are standard medium 55 g and preferably free range and organic.

FLOUR Plain flour is preferably organic. Masa harina is a speciality flour made from maize. It's not at all like cornflour. You could use semolina as a replacement but the flavour would be different. Atta flour is an Indian speciality flour made from split peas.

GARLIC AND GINGER PASTE Garlic and ginger paste is made by simply pureeing garlic or ginger in a food processor with a little oil to loosen to a smooth consistency.

GARLIC AND ONION FLAKES These can be made at home. Finely slice garlic and onion, then gently fry them in some oil at about 150°C until golden. Leave to cool on paper towels. This may seem a little laborious but the results are much better than using flakes you've bought from the supermarket. The pre-cooked flakes you can buy from Chinese supermarkets are okay, but I would advise against buying the Western ones in small glass jars unless absolutely pressed for time.

HERBS I generally use fresh herbs but I've noted where dried herbs are necessary (for example, in rubs and a few sauces). If I have any leftover hard herbs like thyme, sage, rosemary, curry leaves or lime leaves, I like to dry them by simply tying them together with string and hanging them up to dry in a cool, dry place and then storing them in airtight containers. When it comes to oregano, I prefer to use the flowering dried variety, which I call wild oregano.

SALT Maldon is the most widely available quality sea salt but any good-quality crystal salt is fine. Rock salt is always coarse unless otherwise stated. Salt flakes are the same as crystal salt.

TOMATO SAUCE Tomato sauce is generally good old Heinz.

VANILLA SUGAR You can make your own vanilla sugar by storing used dried vanilla pods in sugar over a period of time to allow the flavour to infuse. Alternatively, blend 1 pod with 2 cups of sugar. Either way, vanilla sugar needs to be stored in an airtight container.

INDEX

ACKNOWLEDGEMENTS

This particular book had been waiting for me to write it; I can't believe that it took me so long to get there. It's a style of cooking that has been part of my life since I was a kid. I have to thank Paul McNally for believing in my idea and giving me the support of such a great team, Helen Withycombe, Katri Hilden, photography from Billy Law and great design and typesetting support from Debaser and Transformer, as well as the rest of the team at Hardie Grant.

I could not have managed to write this book without the endless patience of my beautiful wife De-arne. She kept our kiddies from under my feet whilst I was twirling the tongs and hammering out recipes on the computer, as well as helping to clean up after barbecue sessions and parties. To Ruby, Herb and Cash, for being my inspiration and joy.

David, Erica and Jade Anderson for their friendship, support and hospitality. For all you have done for me, thank you. And all my mates who have been subjected to barbecue sessions at my house. Jamie Granger-Smith the only Scouser with a hyphenated name, Antonia, Zac and Benjie, John, Georgia and tribe (you are coming to Australia for a barbecue!). All the other Geordies we know, you know who you are! Those that enjoyed the pig session at the warehouse. Taxi drivers, KPs and chefs whom I have ever worked with, talked about food or consumed it with, you all give me inspiration.

This edition published in 2023 by Hardie Grant Books, an imprint of Hardie Grant Publishing
First published in 2013 as *Ben's BBQ Bible*

Hardie Grant Books (Melbourne)
Wurundjeri Country
Building 1, 658 Church Street
Richmond, Victoria 3121

Hardie Grant Books (London)
5th & 6th Floors
52–54 Southwark Street
London SE1 1UN

hardiegrant.com/books

Hardie Grant acknowledges the Traditional Owners of the Country on which we work, the Wurundjeri People of the Kulin Nation and the Gadigal People of the Eora Nation, and recognises their continuing connection to the land, waters and culture. We pay our respects to their Elders past and present.

A catalogue record for this book is available from the National Library of Australia

BBQ Companion
ISBN 978 1 76145 023 5

10 9 8 7 6 5 4 3 2 1

Publishing Director: Paul McNally, Pam Brewster
Project Editor: Helen Withycombe
Editor: Katri Hilden
Design Manager: Heather Menzies, Kristin Thomas
Designer: Debaser
Cover Designer: Celia Mance
Typesetter: Transformer
Photographer and stylist: Billy Law
Production Manager: Todd Rechner
Production Coordinator: Jessica Harvie

Colour reproduction by Splitting Image Colour Studio
Printed in China by Leo Paper Products LTD

The paper this book is printed on is from FSC®-certified forests and other sources. FSC® promotes environmentally responsible, socially beneficial and economically viable management of the world's forests.